THE MOBIUS GUIDES
the goddess

THE MOBIUS GUIDES

the goddess

TERESA MOOREY

HODDER
MOBIUS

First published in Great Britain in 2003 by Hodder and Stoughton
A division of Hodder Headline

A Mobius paperback

1 3 5 7 9 10 8 6 4 2

A CIP catalogue record for this title is available from the British Library

ISBN 0 34082795 5

Typeset in Fairfield Light by
Palimpsest Book Production Limited, Polmont, Stirlingshire
Printed and bound in Great Britain by
Mackays of Chatham plc, Chatham, Kent

Hodder and Stoughton
A division of Hodder Headline
338 Euston Road
London NW1 3BH

To the Goddess, in all Her forms. May She shine.

Many thanks to my friend Jane Brideson, for encouragement, advice and loan of books! Thanks also to Jane for her wonderful illustrations, in this book and others.

contents

1 why the goddess?   1

  Implications of the loss of the Goddess   2
  Splits and separations   3
  Goddess worship today   5
  Goddess worship as part of a culture   6
  Many forms of deity   6
  Patriarchy in perspective   7
  History   9

2 the ancient great mother   12

  Female images   13
  Caves   15
  Symbols   15
  The earliest myths   18
  The Son-Lover   19
  The Wheel of the Year   21
  Human sacrifice   22
  Sacred sites of earth and stone   23
  Myths and legends   24

3 the triple goddess   29

  The Maiden   30
  The Mother Goddess   33

The Crone   36
Death and rebirth – a fourth aspect   38
The seasons   39
The Moon   40
The Goddess Bride   41

4 the moon goddess   43

The Moon – gifts and associations   45
Lunar effects   47
Lunar festivals   47
Man and the Moon   49
Moon goddesses and myths   50

5 red moon mysteries   53

Prevailing attitudes   54
Tradition and lore   56
Periods and the Moon   58
Shaping our culture   59
The power and poetry of the period   60
Union of opposites   63
Myths and goddesses   64

6 the descent of the goddess   73

Demeter and Persephone   73
Inanna and Ereshkigal   77

7 goddess of many faces   82

Mistress of magic and healing   83
Transcendence   85
Divine protectress – Kuan-Yin   87
The love Goddess – Aphrodite   87
White Buffalo Woman   89

Goddesses of destruction   89
Kali   90
The Valkyries   91
The Warrior Goddess   91
Fertility   92
Lady of the Beasts   93

8 the goddess lives on   98

The Goddess in the Old Testament   99
The New Testament and beyond   102
Into the future   105

further reading and resources   109

1

why the goddess?

Whoso cannot return to the primordial hath no roots in life, but withereth as the grass. These are the living dead who are orphaned of the Great Mother

Dion Fortune, from *The Sea Priestess*

The Feminine has been barely observable within deity over the last 2,000 years. This seems to apply generally to all the major faiths of East and West while the mythology of what we are inclined to call 'more primitive' peoples is consigned to a conceptual hinterland. Where is the Goddess? – and does it matter that She has apparently been lost?

Some would say She hasn't been lost. Deity is really the Great Unmanifest, neither male nor female – or perhaps both male and female. This notwithstanding, God is always called

'He'. It is pointless to say that a pronoun doesn't matter, for words are symbols and they provoke associations in the mind. 'He' means masculinity, and matters are only compounded by the fact that the masculine pronoun is usually used when gender is indistinct, or composite. Others may feel that there is something not quite 'nice' about a Goddess – the age-old association between the Feminine and subversive has not disappeared. We are seeing the ordination of female priests – note, they are not called 'priestesses'! – and while undoubtedly a step in the right direction, there has been violent opposition to this. A memorable quote that female priests should be burnt as witches even appeared in the media – and thereby hangs a tale that we shall be looking at later.

Implications of the loss of the Goddess

What might the loss of our Goddess mean to the world? Firstly, it is sure to mean that women and all things feminine are perceived as inferior. It is hard to see how this could be otherwise. The Virgin Mary, beloved of Catholics, is the established image in the West that is closest to the Goddess, and so important is Mary that the doctrine of her assumption into heaven was declared in the 1940s. There are many traces within Mary of the ancient Great Mother, and to many devout Catholics she is Goddess in all but name. However, her status as Virgin Mother exalts only part of the Feminine, and as a role model she presents an impossibility – a mother who conceived without first having sex. Further than this, Mary is not admitted to the highest honours. She is due extreme veneration, but not adoration, for that is reserved for God. The beautiful image of Mary unfortunately seems to do few favours for women and the Feminine.

Perhaps the most significant implication of the demise of the Goddess has been a loss of a sense of immanence. 'Immanence' implies that deity exists within matter, that all is divine, all sacred.

The ancient Great Mother Goddess not only presided over life – She existed in it. This meant that hill and stream were sacred. It meant that human activities such as weaving, pottery, sowing seeds also were an expression of the sacred, and all existed within a totality – a 'holiness' which means 'wholeness'. The later conception of a Fathergod, existing outside His creation, has emptied the world of life and wonder. It has meant by implication that the world of matter is there to be exploited, and therefore despised, as being set apart from, and lower than, the spiritual abode of God.

The words 'matter' and 'mother' have the same root. It is not hard to see how separation of the divinity from His creation has been bad news for plants, animals, the human body, women and sexuality, not to mention the ecosystem, for what is not divine is flawed and suspect, indeed evil, to be used at will and yet also shunned. The Goddess, who blessed sexual love, whose mystery was revered in each sprouting shoot, was gone. In Her place stood a grass-widower God presiding over a sterile creation.

Splits and separations

The separation of deity from Creation may be seen as a metaphor for the separation of ego-consciousness from a more instinctual condition, where human beings felt themselves to be at one with Earth and cosmos, and where all existed within the Great Mother – we shall explore the Great Mother and Her meanings in Chapter 2. Ego-consciousness meant that individuals were more keenly aware of their uniqueness and their power to effect change in their environment. If this is the case – and we can never be entirely sure about historical processes – then there is little doubt that it has been a necessary phase in human development. In time, however, this would have led to a fear of the old Great Mother, who contained all, amorphously, within Her. As a frail ego fears being swamped by the tide of images from the Unconscious, so a developing sense of Self in humans may have feared the original, instinctual totality. Myths turn the old Goddess into dragon or monster and picture Her defeat by a masculine hero-god. An example of this is the ancient Babylonian goddess Tiamat, dragon-lady of the primordial depths, who is overcome by her great-great-great grandson, Marduk.

The old Goddess embraced both creation and destruction, womb as well as tomb, accepted as a mysterious continuum. To a more detached viewpoint this became incomprehensible. The destructive element was less understood as part of the whole and gradually evolved into an idea of a separate force of evil. A conceptual gulf developed between an idea of good and one of evil, and on either side of this gulf opposite ideas grouped. On the evil side clustered woman, destruction, the body, sex, the earthly – in short all things that had formerly been recognised as necessary and held sacred. Interestingly, as this separation occurred, society, it seems, became more violent, with wars and conquests gaining in momentum. Fear and separation breed conflict.

As the ages passed, evil became personified as Lucifer, the devil, ranged against God. Woman, the flesh and the devil were assembled as a wicked and dangerous package, and a contradiction appeared that has engaged theologians for centuries; for how and why can an omnipotent God tolerate this thorn in His side? Many answers have appeared to this, and some are quite complex. However, to the ancient Goddess worshippers there was no contradiction, only veneration. Creation and destruction are part of a meaningful continuum and both an expression of the Goddess, who makes no bones about being an agent of death as well as life. Interestingly, the belief in a rebellious Satan runs counter to the biblical text 'I form the light and create darkness: I make peace and create evil: I the Lord do all these things' (Isaiah 45:7).

Goddess worship today

Reacceptance of the Goddess could do much to heal splits, encouraging us to face all aspects of our nature and to think deeply before we condemn anyone or anything as 'evil'. However, worship of the Goddess isn't an invitation to do exactly what we like, for it brings an awareness of the cosmic web, and of how each action affects the whole, and affects us. There is no dogma, and the only rule is 'Harm none' but ideally a great deal of personal responsibility is called for.

Paganism, which for the most part is Goddess worship, is enjoying a considerable revival. Some pagan paths are loosely structured, while some, like Wicca, are relatively regimented. All of them exalt the Goddess as at least equal to the God, and even the Northern tradition of the god Odin now has an equal representation of female deities. In addition there are many fiercely feminist pagans who think in terms of the Goddess alone. In a more general sense, there is a considerable number of women who are looking to goddess images and stories as a source of inspiration, while possibly not designating themselves by the term 'pagan'. This makes no difference, for there are no Goddess catechisms to cause agonies of conscience. The Goddess accepts all who come to Her in openness.

Worship of the Goddess is about what you do and feel, about your inner truths, what inspires you, what sends you on journeys of the soul. It is a matter of instinct, encouraging participation and developing mysticism. We have come to think of religion as a set of rules, with right and wrong clearly defined and punishment waiting for those who stray. Goddess worship isn't like that. It lets go of the need for crystallised systems, which instead of creating order have given rise to strife. The Goddess asks that we be true to ourselves, so we may be true to others and true to Her. She blesses our hopes, delights in our pleasures and weaves our losses and our tears on Her loom, so they bring forth meaningful patterns and a certain beauty.

This book is not about any one form of Goddess worship. It concerns the general image of the Goddess and how this has evolved and taken form. If you wish to explore specific paths you may like to read *Witchcraft – a Mobius guide* in this series. These books give more information about different forms of Goddess worship currently available and established.

Goddess worship as part of a culture

The Goddess is not 'God in drag'. She does not sit in the clouds wearing a size 38C breastplate. As in ancient times, She is within us and around us. Exalting the Feminine does not mean merely putting a female at the head of an organisation instead of a male; it means a radical reappraisal of functions and approaches, where greater co-operation is encouraged. There are many ways to be explored in which women can be endowed with greater power and self-determination without feeling that they have to 'become' men. Exploring these ways in a male-dominated status quo can feel forced, and we have to start with truly valuing the feminine qualities that unite rather than differentiate, that accept rather than compete, that receive rather than dictate. It seems we have to feel our way, for we cannot be sure exactly what 'femininity' may be – for instance, there are many warrior goddesses and plenty of room for fierceness within the Feminine. We need to explore – respectfully, trying to drop our old yardsticks.

Many forms of deity

Readers new to the concept of pagan deity may be confused by the fact there are many goddesses, not just one Goddess – and yet there is one, all the same. Pagan ideas support diversity in the Divine as well as the natural world, feeling this holds more potential and colour. The simple fact is that it is up to you. You may think in terms of one Great Mother if you wish, or you may think of many goddesses expressing different functions. You may see all these goddesses as aspects of the One, or you may think in different terms at different times – what matters is what *you* find most inspiring. If your psyche demands neatness, then a single Goddess may serve you best. There isn't a sole 'right' way, but there is a way that is right for you, and this way is your own path to inspiration.

In the following pages we shall be exploring a variety of different goddess myths, taken from Greek, Celtic and other mythologies. These stories come from different eras and they have been chosen to illustrate an aspect of the Goddess – they are not intended to form a chronological picture. Strands of myth weave and interweave, evolving and changing as the centuries progress. Originally, it seems there was one Great Mother Goddess, but not all scholars agree that the 'Goddess of many names' is one Goddess. Many mythologies have a creatrix myth that seems to have gradually diversified into many aspects of the Goddess, including male gods also. In the later pantheons, notably the Greek, the male element becomes more powerful. The Olympian gods of Greece are ruled by Father Zeus, whose Roman counterpart is Jupiter, King of the Gods. In these groupings the goddesses often assume a somewhat inferior role. Nonetheless, the later pantheons have the best-defined stories, and it is usually possible to discern the older, Goddess-orientated pattern, if one looks closely.

Patriarchy in perspective

In the following pages it may seem, at times, that patriarchy and all things male come in for something of an attack. It is difficult to avoid this under the circumstances, but I think we need to remember, surprising though this may sound, that patriarchy has not just been a creation of the human male. As women, we are equal in intelligence to men (and some would say *at least* equal). Although our stamina is greater than men's, our physical strength may not on average match that of men, but the discrepancy is not huge, and there have been warrior traditions for women in many cultures. With this in mind, it seems that somewhere along the line women have acquiesced in the exaltation of maleness, and while a large element of bullying cannot be denied, patriarchy has blown in on the winds of change, somewhere down the aeons. Even today patriarchy is, to a large extent, shored up by women – after all, it is mothers and aunts who hold down the screaming pre-pubescent girls in the infamous practice of female circumcision, and it is they, the women, who cut into that most exquisitely sensitive portion of the female anatomy, the clitoris.

The rage at men, and the rage at patriarchy are undeniable and understandable. The sense of outrage is immense. Hopefully, however, this should not deprive us of a reasonable approach. Individual men are not to blame for the situation, and while many may still support male domination, others are turning in growing numbers to a consciousness of the Goddess, and feeling and expressing a sense of immense sorrow at what has been done to things feminine. In fact, it is doubtful how much men have benefited from patriarchy, for they too have a feminine side, which they have had to bury or amputate, and the 'macho' posing and competition has taken a toll of their health. It is in the interests of all that we retrieve our Goddess, and also that we keep our sense of proportion. The message of the Goddess is about feminine power and it includes savagery and rebellion. But mostly it is about inspiration and awakening to a new consciousness. Men need this too, and so this book is also for men who are interested in Goddess themes.

History

In this book I assume the existence of a predominantly peaceful Stone Age culture, that worshipped the Great Mother for aeons, and we shall begin with this in Chapter 2. For many years it was accepted that history was a linear process of rise and fall, successive races and invasions, and historians produced 'metanarratives' – complete and confident interpretations of the past which also subtly implied certain attitudes to present institutions. Most of us were brought up with the idea of a past more dominated by male aggression than the present – the image of the caveman, club in fist, dragging off his intended mate by her hair lurks in our images of prehistory. However, there is also a feminist metanarrative, expressed most graphically by the archaeologist Marija Gimbutas (see Further Reading) who argues for a woman-centred Europe in the New Stone Age.

In *Lady of the Beasts* (again, see Further Reading) Buffie Johnson tells us: 'The concept of a male God and patriarchal social structures are both comparatively recent developments . . . human society formed itself around the mother and her young, not the father . . . No traces of patriarchal organisation, either in marriage or morality, existed in early culture.' If we look at the whole panorama of history, the priorities of the last 2,000 years are the exception, not the rule. There have been many scholars who have invested belief in a mother-centred, universal Stone Age, Goddess-worshipping culture, that was predominantly peaceful.

Trends these days are towards a very open-minded approach, where students are encouraged to examine the facts and make their own interpretations. Dr Ronald Hutton, professor of History at the University of Bristol, argues fairly, and rather poignantly for this independent approach in a recent edition of *The Ley Hunter*. He says:

. . . acceptable alternatives must exist within the boundaries of the known evidence . . . Even when dealing with the European Neolithic there are limits to the possible. It is perfectly possible, and in some cases very likely, that these cultures were goddess-centred. By contrast, there is absolutely no evidence that any one of them embraced patriarchal monotheism although a lack of data on some areas prevents definitive comment. It is equally possible to suggest that most European Neolithic cultures were female-centred in the social sense, although the data is far more open to differing interpretation. None seem to have been racist, some may well have been egalitarian, some were very artistically creative, and some certainly practised human sacrifice. Most, at least at certain periods, carried on warfare . . . If it was woman-centred, then a woman-centred society is not necessarily opposed to warfare.

No indisputable proof exists concerning universal, peaceful Stone Age worship of the Great Mother, and although many of us would like to say it does and raise the declaration as a feminist banner, to do so would be to create another, different dogma, potentially as damaging as the dogmas of Fathergod. So, in fairness, I must say that my presentation of a universal Great Mother is in some cases subjective – although some would argue otherwise, including several books in 'Further Reading'. From my point of view it is a wonderful story, and it is a truth, if not *the* truth. Certainly it is my truth. Perhaps by regarding the past in this way we may give ourselves hope for the future, and conjure into our world the in-dwelling beauty and awe of the Goddess.

Practice

As we embark on our exploration of the Goddess and Her meanings, perhaps you would like to take the time to think about all this implies. What might reinstatement of the Feminine mean? What, in fact, is the Feminine? In what ways have feminine-related matters been neglected, despised, persecuted? How might matters be improved by Goddess worship? What is your own favourite image of the Goddess, and what does She mean to your life? Perhaps you have more than one image. What was your relationship like with your personal mother? How might a more matriarchal culture or a powerful Goddess image have helped matters? Was your mother able to mediate strong and complete models of the Feminine for you? If not, where do you think these may have been lacking? — for example, were women assumed to be dependent to men, necessarily mothers, destined only for certain roles in life, etc? Make a note, if you like, of all the things that seem important to you.

2

the ancient
great mother

I am she who ere the earth was formed
Was Ea, Binah, Ge
I am that soundless, boundless, bitter sea
Out of whose deeps life wells eternally . . .

Invocation from, *The Sea Priestess* by Dion Fortune

Down the misty aeons of the Stone Age, the ancient Great Mother reigned alone. It is tantalising to imagine those times – rituals of the hunt, stories woven in firesmoke at the cave mouth, the dreams of a forgotten people. But in the secrecy of our body wisdom they are remembered, coded in our DNA, and when at night we leave our world of manufactured comfort, we enter theirs, in our dreams.

We are used to assuming, smugly, that the passage of time means progress, that the present is always better, more advanced than the past, and that the longer ago something took place the more rudimentary and ignorant it must have been. That isn't necessarily the case. It may have been that prehistoric humans knew a thing or two. The psychologist Carl Gustav Jung stated that the combined history and experience of mankind was contained within the unconscious mind, and that below the layers of everyday awareness lay many strata of knowledge from generation upon generation. This means that the personality is rather like an archeological dig, or an iceberg, with much hidden under the surface. Somewhere deep within us lies the cavewoman and caveman, and perhaps these people did more than wave clubs and grunt. Perhaps they hold the key to some things we have lost.

The first image of life identified by humanity was, it seems, the Mother. Logically, the Supreme Being seemed undeniably feminine, for birth belonged to Her, and so by extension, death and rebirth also. The female body holds within the mystery of birth, which, by analogy, is the mystery of the unseen becoming manifest throughout the cosmos – so Mother, with all attendant meanings, becomes the mystery of life itself. This image, enshrined in art, comes down to us from probably as early as 20,000 BCE, develops through the Bronze Age and Iron Age and still exists, to some extent, today.

Female images

Many female figures have been unearthed, hewn in mammoth ivory, bone or stone. These often have enlarged belly or buttocks suggesting pregnancy, with abundant, pendulous breasts and generous thighs. Some of the best-known examples of these are the Goddess of Laussel, a carving 43 cm high, from the Dordogne in France dating from c.22,000–18,000 BCE; the

Goddess of Willendorf, Austria, a limestone statue, 11 cm tall (c.20,000–18,000 BCE); and the fired clay goddess from Dolni Vestonice, Czechoslovakia, dating from a similar period, 11.5 cm tall.

These are rooted, solid figures with a strange and powerful ambience, epitomising awe at the creative process. We can hear their magnificent story, if we will listen. Similar male figures have not been unearthed. These are not mere figures of women, for they embody the drama of birth – they have the aura of the sacred. Many figures were painted with red ochre, the colour of life. Some were made with legs tapering to a point, presumably so they could be transported when necessary, then planted in the ground for ritual or worship.

Caves

Not surprisingly caves were seen as the womb of the earth Goddess. Baring and Cashford (see Further Reading) tell us:

> *The story of a great primeval goddess is told in the caves of south-western France, through the art and rituals that took place inside them. For at least 20,000 years (from 30,000 to 10,000 bc) the Palaeolithic cave seems to be the most sacred place, the sanctuary of the Goddess and the source of her regenerative power . . . To those who would have lived in a sacred world, the actual hollow shape would have symbolised her all-containing womb, which brought forth the living and took back the dead.*

The courage of religious fervour must have inspired these people to wriggle through subterranean passages, sometimes over a mile, into the belly of the earth, in order to decorate vast underground chambers with sacred imagery. Stalactites were painted with dots, to represent breasts, and everywhere around the walls ran and leaped the wild animals of the era, showing forth the power of the Goddess. The female animals appear to have been given pride of place in these chambers, that were no doubt the scene of wondrous rituals.

Symbols

Many symbols were used in relation to the Goddess. Connection of life cycles with the Moon, discussed in a later chapter, were observed by the cave dwellers. The Moon is represented symbolically by the bison's horn, held by the Goddess of Laussel, and notches were often marked in sets of seven to denote the days of the four lunar quarters.

Chevron

The chevron was an important symbol, for it suggested bird and water. The bird was one of the earliest Goddess-messengers, appearing apparently from nowhere out of the sky and linking earth, sea and sky with its powers and flight. In addition, birds such as vultures that fed on corpses were seen as agents of rebirth. The egg, laid by the bird, was a sign of rebirth, and figures of goddesses with large buttocks, as if holding an egg, have been discovered in numbers. Many creation myths tell of a World Egg laid by the Goddess, and creation can be seen as emerging miraculously from the egg, as a baby bird does. Certain birds may dive for food, disappearing underwater for some time, only to soar anew from the depths. Water was seen as the source of all life, as the waters in the womb. Both bird with outspread wings and waves upon water are rendered by chevrons and zig-zags, so giving them a sacred meaning.

Spiral

The spiral, too, is a shape made by eddying water. The spiral represents the entry into and out of manifestation that occurs at birth and death, and which suggests rebirth continuity and mystery. The spiral is a recurrent motif in connection with the Goddess, linking later with the similar theme of the Labyrinth, in Crete. By a similar token, the spiral also means initiation into hidden knowledge – a type of death and rebirth. The serpent, a beast of many meanings, is also suggested by the meander/ spiral. Serpents were sacred to the Goddess for millenia, debased as the one who tempted Eve. The spiral is also the form for a ritual dance, and is recognised in the popular symbols of present-day Goddess worshippers.

Triangle

The triangle was also used to represent the Goddess, and can be seen as a containing chalice, or as signifying the genitals. Triangles, meanders and chevrons have been found carved on bone figures from c.30,000–20,000 BCE.

Net

The net also appears with symbolic meaning, from the Palaeolithic era onwards. The cosmos can be seen as a net, containing all life, Later images show goddesses spinning or weaving life on a loom and this connection prevailed even with the Virgin Mary, who is depicted as spinning, in an Upper Rhenish painting, c. 1400 CE. This painting shows Mary, the Divine Child in her womb, the thread from her spindle passing through the brow of the child, into her hands. Here we can trace in Mary the image of the Creatrix. Many of the very earliest activities, such as sowing seeds, making pottery, spinning and weaving are laden with sacred metaphor, for in earlier times all life processes were held sacred, all were a part of the Goddess, and most were practised by women. This consciousness of sacred living has been retained to this day by the native Americans.

Knot

Extending from the net, the knot, favoured by Cretan priest-esses, signifies mystery. The Cretan culture worshipped the goddess in apparently uninterrupted peace, showing an unbroken progression from the Neolithic into the Bronze Age, and retaining an image of the unity of life and its vivid joy. The priestess/goddess figure from Crete, wearing a characteristic bell-shaped skirt, holds serpents in either hand, above breasts gloriously bared. When we look at a knot we cannot see the entirety – we know that connections are made, meaningful complications exist which we cannot encompass in a glance. Like the spiral and labyrinth, the knot can signify passage into the visible world and out of it. It also has links with the reed bundles of the Sumerian goddess Inanna. Even today it is still fashionable for women to wear a knotted scarf about the neck, and sober-suited businessmen wear ties – often in bright colours. Could this be an oblique compliment to the Goddess?

Ankh

A symbol well known from Ancient Egypt is the ankh. The ankh also may be seen as a knot. It, too, is interpreted as the union of male and female, with the femine loop above the masculine cross. In addition, it may represent the female genitals, or the menstrual napkin of the goddess Isis.

The earliest myths

It is probable that ancient humans lived within a mystical dreamtime, with an ever-present sense of meaning and totality. Contained within the womb of the Great Mother, each felt her or himself to be part of something greater. Rebirth was not a promise, it was a reality. The Mother Goddess held all, cause and effect, event and explanation, life and death within Her. She produced, transformed and endured. The dead were returned to Her, in order that She might return them, in some way, to life.

However, living within this continuum is different from being an agent of change within it. Humans were not just part of life and death: to live they had to be the cause of death to other creatures. This may have presented them with a paradox and a threat, for once the continuum is felt to be ruptured then death becomes frightening, and separation and loss become a reality. This may be one of the aspects of the idea of 'fall from grace'.

And so, to the all-embracing myth of the Great Mother the hunter myth grew up – rituals for he who must kill and violate the oneness. The practice of shamanism grew, which is a purposeful attempt, in effect, to preserve the mystical unity and to channel the Divine into the here-and-now. Cashford and Baring tell us: 'The goddess myth contains the hunter myth, but the hunter myth cannot contain the goddess myth'. The caves, with their paintings inside, represent this containment of one myth by the other, and no doubt complex rites surrounded the hunt, to preserve unity and to venerate the spirits of the animals slain.

The Son-Lover

The Palaeolithic Great Mother is almost androgynous. Represented at times in figures as having a long, bird-like neck, this neck can also be seen as phallic. The male role in procreation may not have been realised, and so the womb must have seemed almost a magical place of generation. The earliest depiction of the masculine in relation to the Goddess was in the shape of animals, and these were an outpouring, a manifestation of Her dynamic power. In this respect the bull is one of the best known, and it is interesting that a cross-section of womb and ovaries looks like a bull's head. This would have been observed, as corpses were often exposed, to be consumed by vultures. A shrine uncovered in Catal Huyuk, Turkey, c.6500 BCE shows the Mother Goddess giving birth to a bull's head, with horns.

In the Neolithic era humanity discovered a new way to participate in the mysteries of growth, in the discovery of agriculture. As the climate grew warmer and the glaciers retreated, two million years of hunting animals and gathering fruit was superseded gradually, yet radically, by agrarian culture. Women presided over the sowing, growing, harvest and storage of crops, for women were the carriers of life and could best embody the sacred link between the seen and unseen. Images of the Goddess became more intricate, and She was also seen as Vegetation Goddess. However, as the Neolithic progressed into the Bronze Age, the image of the God became more defined.

The masculine image took shape as the Son-Lover of the Goddess, to whom She gave birth each year, who grew to maturity, mated with Her and impregnated Her, died cut down with the harvest and falling with the leaves, sojourned in the Underworld and was later reborn as His own Son. In this respect the Goddess is seen as the entirety of the seasonal cycle embracing Earth and cosmos. The God is He Who Travels – He is the Son/Sun, who grows, dies and is 'reborn' during the year. He is the life-force and He is the seed and the plant that also grows and dies.

Some feminists have called the value of this image into question, stating that it stems from patriarchy and the de-potentising of women who then have to live out their lives through envied and adored sons. However, it is rather a way of differentiating between male and female energies, seeing them as conjoined, cyclical, interdependent. Nor does it sanction incest, whether actual or psychical. The union of Goddess and God was celebrated in the sacred sexual act – the 'sacred marriage' – which was seen as taking place between king and land. It was from the land herself that the king derived his power, and his symbolic mating with the High Priestess, representative of the Goddess, acknowledged and blessed this fact.

The Wheel of the Year

The 'Wheel of the Year' is the seasonal cycle, arranged into eight festivals, telling the 'story' of the Goddess and Her Son-Lover, the God. This is observed in growing numbers by people who wish to retrieve a more ancient relationship with the Earth and with Nature. Based mainly on ancient Celtic festivals, the Wheel begins with the Celtic New Year at Samhain, or Hallowe'en, on 31 October, for to the Celts darkness meant beginnings. At Samhain the Goddess is Crone, wise and alone, while the God is Underworld Lord. At Yule (around 21 December) He is born again as Divine Child of the Mother Goddess. At Imbolc (2 February) the Goddess is celebrated in all Her forms, and the Spring Equinox (around 20 March) is a festival of burgeoning vegetation, while the Goddess and God are growing to maturity. Their union is celebrated at Beltane, 31 April, perhaps the greatest of the fertility festivals, and the year culminates with the Midsummer Solstice, around 21 June.

Now the God begins slowly to recede and He is cut down with the harvest at Lammas (31 July). The harvest is finally celebrated at the Autumn Equinox, around 23 September, and so to Samhain again.

This story can be told in a variety of ways and has paradoxes and overlaps. Behind it lies a vision of life as created by the sexual act, and explicitly defines sexuality as sacred. This viewpoint is not generally popular in our culture, but it is interesting that a slang word for intercourse – a 'bang' – is used to describe the creation story that is currently favoured – the 'Big Bang' theory!

Some people prefer the story to be one of the changing aspects of the Goddess alone. While this is a very ancient tradition it is evolving currently in a variety of different ways. To discover more you may like to consult *The Wheel of the Year – Myth and Magic Throughout the Seasons*, published by Hodder & Stoughton (see Further Reading).

Human Sacrifice

Ancient culture is often dismissed as barbaric, and while this is often highly debatable (and begging definition), there is no doubt that human sacrifice was practised at certain times and places. Animal sacrifice was popular in many cultures, and we can observe its vestiges in bull-fighting, for the bull was a favoured choice of animal.

Present-day pagans often make offerings to the earth, such as herbs, crumbs or wine, given at certain times and/or at special locations. However, the spirit behind this is one of recognition, thanks and festivity. This is very different from the fear that underlies much sacrifice.

Cruelty is usually bred by fear of some sort, and we can trace the beginnings of fear back to the separation from the primal oneness enjoyed by primitive humans. In a state of mystical unity there is no fear, for all is experienced as meaningful and containing – this is attested by present-day mystics. The polarisation of desire – that impression of subject and object, of being apart from the thing or person that you want – is resolved by the notion of an indwelling deity that informs all. Perception of this 'indwellingness' is mysticism, and Goddess worship encourages personal revelation and suggests a resolution of the desire conflict by emphasising immanence – although, of course, there are mystics of all faiths. Feeling that you are 'at one' with creation produces bliss and trust.

As human ego-consciousness advanced, so the mystical unity receded, and this was no doubt an unavoidable step on the evolutionary path. Along with separation grew anxiety. This was not just the fear of being 'lost' but also a sensation that loss of the 'oneness' was a violation of the sacred. And the sacred continuum was also ruptured by the hunting and killing of animals.

It is not hard to see that being afraid may produce a need to make reparation for perceived crimes. Perhaps a crippled form of recognising one's part in the continuum is feeling the need to 'repay' (for generosity that one might not merit, or might cease). It is also comfortable to have someone to blame – hence, the 'scape-goat'. From these dynamics it is likely that sacrifice of humans and animals was adopted. Where there is anxiety, there may also be the fear that the bounty of the deity will be withdrawn. If a bull/cock/human isn't sacrified, to drip blood upon the fields, then maybe next year the crops won't grow, or the Sun will not return after winter's chill. War can also be seen as ritual sacrifice, per-haps as a subconscious drive. It has been suggested that human sacrifice was not practised by the matrifocal cultures, but was a later patriarchal innovation. The Goddess is Death Mother, but Her worship does not demand sacrifice, She asks that we accept and try to understand, as we are contained within Her accept-ance, for Her 'love is poured out upon the earth'.

Sacred sites of earth and stone

During the latter part of the Neolithic era, around 5000 BCE, great circles of stone were erected. The effort and time involved in building these is incalculable, and there can be little doubt that only the spiritual urge, defined by Jung as basic to human life, was the driving force. These circles are complex structures marking the motions of Sun and Moon, and many are well known, such as Stonehenge, Avebury, Callanish and Carnac. In addition, there are countless earthworks, linking earth and sky in holy metaphor. Two examples of these are New Grange in Northern Ireland, and the barrow at Stony Littleton in Avon. At the time of the Midwinter Solstice at Yule, season of death and rebirth, the bright fingers of the returning Sun penetrate deep into the wombs of earth, awakening and impregnating her, and she welcomes his return.

Such earthworks have often been described as tombs, but this may be missing the point, and is similar to calling our present-day churches, with their graveyards, 'tombs'. These were sacred sites, whose power was sensed by a people still sensitive to the currents of energy networking the surface of the Earth. The dead were returned to their home in these special sites, to the tomb that was also womb, to await rebirth from the all-generating earth-mother. So the earth is death mother and birth mother. The Goddess deals out death when this must be and promises birth in due season, and the earth embodies this promise.

Myths and Legends

We can only piece together the early legends of the Great Mother from stone and bone fragments that have been left to us. For picturesque narrative we have to turn to more defined sources that came later. One of the early Greek creatrix figures was the Goddess Eurynome.

Eurynome dances the world alive

Most ancient of deities, great Eurynome rose naked from Chaos and began to dance. As she danced, so light separated from darkness and sea from sky. On and on she whirled, in ecstasy, creating in her wake a wind that grew lustful towards her. Turning towards the wind she grasped it in her hands and shaped it into the serpent, Ophion. Eurynome and Ophion had intercourse, and then, in the shape of a dove, Eurynome laid the World Egg, from which hatched all that lives. Some myths say that Ophion hatched the egg. Others go on to tell how Ophion grew arrogant and bragged that he was the origin of all, whereupon Eurynome threw him down into the Underworld, retaining her supreme position. We may see in the myth of Eurynome the creative essence of movement, still practised today by shamans as they dance into the world of manifestation what they have experienced in Otherworld. To the later Greeks Eurynome took on a reduced significance as a sea deity.

Spider woman

In the south-west of North America, the Zuni and the Hopi saw the Goddess as a great, big-bodied spider. Legend tells how Grandmother Spider took some earth and mixed it with saliva to form the first living beings. She covered them with a magical white cape, made from Creative Wisdom and sang over them her Creation Song. These two beings took up complementary roles – the one solidified the earth while the other, called 'Echo', had the function of making the world resonate to the forces of creation. This myth, from the other side of the globe, complements that of Eurynome, using the generative power of sound, as Eurynome uses dance. They are both lovely metaphors for the creative value of 'play'.

Isis and Osiris

Great Isis, Goddess of Egypt, has been described as the most complete goddess form ever evolved. Although not precisely a 'creatrix' she embodies all aspects of divinity, and many of the other Egyptian goddesses can be seen as different faces of Isis. Hathor, the winged cow goddess, said to have given birth to the world in some myths, is one of the personifications of Isis, for both goddesses wear a crown of cow's horns with the Sun's disk resting between them. Isis is also portrayed wearing the throne as crown, for it was from her authority the pharoahs drew their power of kingship.

Isis was born from Nut, the great sky goddess, who lay over

her husband Geb, the earth – this is an interesting departure from the more usual format of sky-father and earth-mother. Along with Isis were born Osiris, Seth and Nephthys. Nephthys became wife to Seth while Osiris wed Isis and together they ruled Egypt. However Seth, the dark brother, grew jealous of the popularity of Osiris. During an evening of festivity he tricked Osiris into lowering himself into a jewelled chest, which was then nailed down and pushed out into the Nile, to be carried out to sea. At length it came to rest on the Phoenician coast, beneath a tamarisk tree. The local king cut down the tree to be used in the construction of his palace, but it gave off such a marvellous scent that news of it travelled far and wide, reaching the ears of sorrowing Isis. By her knowledge of magic Isis knew what this meant and she set out at once to retrieve it.

Weeping over the body of her beloved, Isis through her magical arts conceived their child, Horus. She hid the precious chest in the remote reaches of the Nile delta, and struggled as a lone mother to bring up Horus. From this Isis comes to exemplify all the loving aspects of motherhood which are retold in other myths about her, and we can see her as a goddess who understands human suffering. Meanwhile, however, Seth had not given up. Retrieving the coffin he cut the corpse of Osiris into fourteen pieces – we see here links with the half-cycle of the Moon, of about fourteen days. Now Isis had the macabre task of retrieving the pieces of her husband's body, and gradually arms, legs and internal organs were found among bullrushes or embedded in swamps. Thirteen pieces were reassembled, but the fourteenth, the phallus of Osiris, had been swallowed by a fish. By her art Isis reconstructed this, fanning the body with her great wings so that Osiris revived, to become king of the Underworld. Horus grew up to avenge his father on his uncle, Seth.

Osiris is a form of the vegetation god that comes to life in the rising waters of the Nile and dies as it falls and the grain withers. Horus, his son, is really another aspect of him, and so he is an example of the Son-Lover god, while Isis is the Great Mother. Nephthys, wife to Seth, is shown helping Isis and is another aspect of her – Isis is the dawn, Nephthys the twilight. Despite their bitter conflict, Seth is in a sense a part of Osiris. He is the dark twin who overcomes the light at the Midsummer Solstice, heralding the retreat of the Sun. At Yule, the Midwinter Solstice, Osiris/Horus defeats Seth – although these dates are not appropriate for Egypt, the concept coincides. These two aspects are sometimes called the Oak King of the Waxing Year and the Holly King of the Waning Year. Throughout the cycle Isis presides, rejoicing, bewailing, healing, transform-ing, giving birth and also destroying, for myth tells how Isis in mourning dealt death from her divine eyes. Isis is a great god-dess indeed, and it was from her rites that the mystery cult of Eleusis is said to have evolved.

We may call Isis into our lives by spreading our arms, like her wings, and standing tall. Do this in sunlight or moonlight, take a few deep breaths and draw the energy of the air deep within you, feeling it tingling along your veins. Isis shows us how a woman can stand alone, stand tall, asking no one's permission to be who she is, and yet at the same time having the courage to feel and to nurture. Feel the blessing of Great Isis spread all over you in a glow of warmth.

Practice

For our practice let us return to the ancient Stone Age goddess and attempt to rediscover Her in earthworks and stone circles. How you do this is up to you. Many people feel these sites of antiquity have many powers, and you may experience this for yourself if you approach in a spirit of open-minded reverence. Go at twilight, go in mist and storm, when few if any other people will be abroad. Empty your mind and give yourself time to daydream — what images occur to you? How do you feel? What physical sensations do you experience? Take a candle with you and enter the black depths of a chosen earthwork (needless to say, you should ensure that this is safe). Earthworks are sites of death and rebirth; many women experience feelings of sexual arousal at such places, and earthworks have also been described as shamanic gateways by Danny Sullivan, editor of The Ley Hunter magazine. Simply, these are transformative places, where we may experience Otherworld in some fashion. Legend also says that the fairy people of the Sidhe, led by their pale, shimmering queen, ride forth from these mounds on moonlit nights. You may be surprised what enchantment they may reveal to you.

3

the triple goddess

Behold the Three-Formed Goddess
She who is ever Three – Maid, Mother and Crone;
Yet is she ever One.
For without Spring there can be no Summer,
Without Summer, no Winter,
Without Winter, no new Spring

Wiccan Goddess Invocation

Three is often considered to be a special number. It appears in folklore and fairy tales as three wishes, three special encounters, three chances, three gifts. To many people three is lucky. The triangle is a magical shape, and three is sometimes called the number of generation, being Mother, Father and Child, for the two has brought forth a third. Many factors assemble in threes – mind, body, spirit; past, present, future, and so on – it has a feeling of balance. In astrological terms, the trine aspect is linked to flow, harmony, and the idea of a Holy Trinity is well known in Christianity. The cosmos is contemplated in three parts – upper, middle and lower – and it may be because of this that the Ancient Goddess is so often seen as triple.

There are many groupings of three goddesses in mythology. Scandinavian belief told of three Norns living beneath the World Tree – these were fateful goddesses against whom even the mighty Aesir were powerless. Greek myth tells of three Fates, three Furies (Erinyes) and the three-times-three band of nine Muses. Indeed, many single goddesses can be perceived to be triple upon investigation – Hecate, for instance and most notably, Celtic Bride.

The Triple Goddess is seen as Maiden, Mother and Crone, thereby enshrining all seasons of femininity. It is easy to revere the Mother, for she is exalted in our tradition. Mothers bring forth babies – we all have a mother, and we are all encouraged to show respect for her. Motherhood is the most 'respectable' face of the feminine to a society within which dynasty and pro-creation are pre-eminent. However, for women to be restricted to a motherly role model is to hamper, most severely, the potential of the Feminine.

The Maiden

We are familiar with the idea of a maiden as meaning the same as 'virgin' – a young woman who has not had sexual intercourse. However, the meaning here has been given a twist that is quite misleading. 'Virgin' originally meant belonging to no one other than oneself. The virgins of the ancient goddess temples would often have sex with male travellers, for they were represen-tatives of the Goddess, participating in one of Her sacred acts.

However, they belonged to no man – they were independent, self-possessed, giving themselves where they wished and bound by no imposed rules. The Maiden is untamed woman, wild, free, vibrant with energy, unpredictable as the wind. Her response to life is spontaneous, vivid. She is sexual, yes, and highly seductive, but to some extent her sexuality is focused on exploration, and a fascination with her own womanhood. She will give delight, but not commitment. Her lovers adventure with her, but they certainly never, ever own her. This intensifies her allure, of course, and may be very uncomfortable for a certain type of masculine consciousness, bent on conquest. The Maiden in part embodies certain characteristics that have been reserved unfairly for men – she may be sexually free, but she is utterly feminine. She loves where she wills and proudly guards the sanctity of her own body. The Maiden aspect of the Goddess may feel most vivid at the festivals of Imbolc, Spring Equinox and Beltane.

We see the Maiden in mini-skirted, leather-jacketed girls who are tasting what life has to offer, exploring their power as individuals and females, forming their own thoughts on life, The Maiden is fairly objective. However beautiful she may be, her urge is not so much to relate, but more to assess, experience and find her own forms of order – the underlying motive here is better knowledge of the self. We call upon the Maiden whenever we enter uncharted territory in our work, self-knowledge or relationships. We need her fresh vision and healthy self-centredness at all phases of our lives. Young girls, who are naturally close to the Maiden, need to be encouraged to use their energies in ways that are likely to develop their sense of individuality to the full, to be true to themselves, for only in that way will they be able to be true to anything, or anyone else. Older women may have been cramped or repressed in their youth, and they may need to reclaim the Maiden, consciously, to free their spirits and find their direction. Many a midlife crisis is wrought by a Maiden, cloistered and confined, rushed too early into a conventional marriage, with no chance to explore alternatives in sexuality or career. Young women on motorbikes, in laboratories, studying gorillas in the wild, striding on the stage, declaiming on the political platform – they are wonderful, they are Maiden. Breathe her in and let her brighten your eyes.

Myth and Legend – Artemis

Like many goddesses, Artemis has multiple attributes, and although she has come down to us, depicted in art as the virgin moon-goddess, it is probable that she, as with many goddesses, originally embodied all aspects of the Great Mother. Her name comes from the word for 'bear'. Bear is a powerful totem of earthy wisdom, for bears know where to find the roots and herbs that will heal, and they incubate their young in hibernation, throughout the cold of winter. As warrior goddess she was patroness of the Amazons, as the many breasted Artemis of Ephesus, she embodied fecundity. She was also guardian of women in childbirth. There is no contradiction here – as 'virgin' goddess all women's matters were her fierce concern. She it was who slew with her merciless arrows any huntsman who pursued pregnant females, or their young. She embodied the law of Nature, the ruthless, ancient order of the wildwood. Her festivals were celebrated on nights of the Full Moon, in forest clearings, in a rapture where boundaries dissolved and where human became one with Nature and Goddess in orgiastic, anonymous mating.

Artemis was one of the few deities over whom Aphrodite, the love-goddess, had no power. Myth tells of the huntsman Actaeon, who came upon the lovely goddess while she was bathing. Seeing her he was transfixed, motionless. She was so beautiful, personifying all the Earth's primeval power, and yet ethereal and enchanting. Artemis saw him, and with a flash of her proud eyes turned him into a stag. Actaeon's own hounds then set upon him and tore him to pieces. (We can see here echoes of the Horned God of the animals, and the vegetation deity, who dies of his love for the Goddess, and is reborn each spring.)

And so, while Artemis may bless acts of love and pleasure, she is not to be tamed, or intruded upon. Women may call on her when they need all available self-assertion or independence. Artemis is near in all wild, uninhabited places. Seek her far from the beaten track, in the company of her animals; seek her face in leaf and stone, breathe her in with the scent of the soil, and ride with her on the wind.

The Mother Goddess

'Mother' is the most acceptable face of the Feminine, and while she has not, over the last 2,000 years in the Western world, been part of the concept of deity, yet we see echoes of the ancient Mother Goddess in Mary, the mother of Jesus. To many Catholics Mary is Goddess, to the emotions and to the soul, and she fulfils what the author Geoffrey Ashe terms the 'goddess-shaped yearning' although the canons of the Church deny her divine status. Mary exemplifies all the love, devotion, gentleness, responsiveness and caring that motherhood encompasses. In a world where the natural instincts of many mothers have been cramped, along with other aspects of their being, many of us feel we have been deprived, to some extent, of mother love. The loving arms of the Mother are what we all yearn for.

The Mother gives birth to, and blesses, all of life. Babies, animals, flowers, crystals, all flow from her divine womb. In spring she opens her earth-body to give birth to bright, new growth. In summer she enfolds protective arms around the glowing land. At harvest time she spreads wide her bounty, and as the cold takes hold, she snuggles the wintering animals in their dens, drawing the seeds deep within her belly until the greening time again arrives. She is productive, giving, nourishing – the Milky Way spills from her flowing breasts and glistens through the galaxy. She listens, responds, takes care and counsels – but although she may sometimes be firm, her counsels are usually gentle.

The Maiden may inspire our creative acts, but the Mother is there as we produce them. She stands behind each physical mother, supporting, encouraging, loving – and mothers may mediate her to their children. She also comforts mothers who have lost, for the Great Mother loses her Son-Lover, the God of dying and resurrecting Nature, and each winter she must mourn him, until He returns in spring. Sorrowing Mary, beneath Christ's cross, partakes of this. The Mother Goddess is a comfort also to mothers who feel they are not good enough in their role – with her understanding and support they may retrieve, inwardly, some of the succour that would have been more generally available in the days of matriarchal tribes, when women were not isolated but had grandmothers to turn to for advice. The Mother is equally important to women who do not have physical children, either through choice or necessity. She expands and blesses all their creative acts and endows them with the tranquil thoughtfulness that is so culturally valuable. The Mother is our inward blessing. Bathe in her grace, at full Moon's light, and rejoice with her as you smell summer flowers, or eat newly baked bread.

Myth and Legend – Demeter

Almost all goddesses represent the fertile aspect of the Feminine in some way, for even with the virginal goddesses, such as Athene, Germanic Eostre and Artemis we see attributes of fertility, protectiveness, mistress of the household and such like. However, we turn again to Greek mythology once more, for a supreme picture of motherhood – giving, tending, sorrowing and rejoicing – in the person of Demeter.

'Earth Mother' is one of the meanings of Demeter's name, and she was worshipped with natural offerings, such as honeycombs, grain and fresh fruit. She may be seen as the corn goddess, spreading wide her golden cloak on the fields. It is Demeter who keeps the earth fruitful and fertile. Legend tells of her loving bond with her daughter Persephone, who is abducted by the Underworld god, Hades (or Pluto). For Demeter, the tragic loss is overwhelming. Anyone who has a child knows that the worst imaginable grief is to lose the child, and Demeter scours the land, wringing her hands and calling her daughter, and weeping. Again, we see the mother-child story of the seasons, but with Demeter it is a daughter who 'dies' and resurrects, not a son, and with this legend the cycle of the seasons is explained in wholly feminine terms. We may remember the Goddess chiefly as Mother at Midsummer, Lammas and Yule.

As Demeter mourns, all is neglected, and the first winter claws at the land. Men and beasts die, and the gods in Olympus begin to fear their worshippers will all be exterminated. So negotiations take place to return Persephone to the upper air. Because she has eaten of the pomegranate – a fertility symbol – Persephone cannot leave the Underworld permanently, and she is always known as the Underworld Queen. However, she returns to her mother for eight months of the year, and this is when the land blossoms. During the remaining four months she must return to her dark lover. Her mother sorrows, and winter comes – we notice here that the Greek winter is shorter than the British one!

It is interesting that during her time of mourning and searching, Demeter spends time, disguised as a nurse, in the court of Eleusis. While there she tries to make the little prince, Triptolemus, immortal, by immersing him in fire, but she is interrupted by his mother, and has to reveal her divinity. This maternal intervention shows how our human restricted perspectives often frustrate us in search of the Divine. The figure of Triptolemus is expanded in subsequent myths to take on almost the stature of vegetation deity, Son-Lover to the goddess, and it was in Eleusis that the Mystery cult grew. By her attempt to give eternal life to the boy by burning him we see the power of the goddess as life-in-death, death-in-life, and this was one of the focal themes of the Eleusinian Mysteries.

Originally, Demeter seems to have arisen from the identity of the Great Mother herself. We may draw close to Demeter in any field or garden. If we are tired, sorrowful, lonely or merely meditative, or if we are conscious of our own lack of personal mothering, the motherliness of Demeter surrounds us, in the embrace of Nature, and we can absorb a sense of peace.

The Crone

While the Maiden is sought and the Mother revered, the figure of the Crone receives scant attention. In our culture old women are often neglected and even insulted, and the gifts they represent, and often have to offer, are not valued. Old age may be dreaded as a loss of attractiveness in a male-dominated society that values women only for their seductiveness and fertility. However, it is in the Crone that feminine power truly comes into its own.

The Crone is wise one, watcher, weaver, healer and shaper. We may picture her in her cottage or cave, musing, brewing, muttering. She closely resembles the picture of the witch, so increasing the suspicion with which she is viewed. The Crone knows the ways between the worlds and so she understands all too well the ways of this world. This can make her an uncomfortable personage, but she is the repository of female wisdom, of the accumulated knowledge of the woman who no longer menstruates, but holds within herself the store of her power.

We have come to the Crone last in our trio, but to the Celts the Crone came first, before Maiden, for the Crone is darkness, and it was the darkness that existed first, in the primeval void, before the light was brought forth. Knowing the value of darkness, the Celts began their day at nightfall, their year in autumn, at the feast of Samhain, or Hallowe'en, and Crone was remembered before bright Maiden, so giving pride of place to her unutterable wisdom. Her presence creeps in at the Autumn Equinox and deepens our sense of winter.

The Crone is our source of wisdom and understanding. She is mistress of lore, all the stored learning of generation upon generation of ancestors. She knows the ways of magic, she understands transformation and she spins the cosmic web, knowing that all is part of the whole. She may be the kindly, rosy-cheeked granny in her herb garden, or she may be the shadow-haunting hag. The wisdom of the Crone is sometimes gentle and sometimes abrasive, for she shows us how to relate to the universe and to our deeper selves. She is there in the whisper of the leaf and the growl of the storm. We can go to her whenever we know we need to change, or when we seek deep understanding of any matter.

Myth and Legend – Cailleach

Usually referred to as 'the Cailleach', this is a strongly drawn Celtic form of the Crone goddess, who is unutterably ancient. It was said that she could renew herself endlessly, reverting to the prime of life to take a new lover, as her current one died of old age. She is sometimes pictured stirring her cauldron of death and rebirth, in the Underworld. However, we may also see her striding through a grey landscape, carrying boulders in her apron, for her strength is uncanny. As cosmic goddess she rules the weather, sky and seasons. Her teeth are red and her hair matted. Her face, the blue-black colour of a lake beneath storm clouds, has one central eye. There are few myths written about

37

her but she is echoed in ancient place names. It is likely that she was goddess of the old, pre-Celtic peoples, the dwellers of the hollow hills, and so she is an eerie goddess in truth.

Story tells how Cailleach owned a farm, taking on many labourers, on the condition that they would be paid only if they could out-work her. One look at her wizened form convinced most that they had easy pickings. They were rewarded by an early death, from exhaustion, trying in vain to match her phenomenal powers. Cailleach would cackle over their corpses – in her we have a metaphor for the immense strength of the old woman, that is usually not perceived, but can move mountains, as easily as Cailleach did, dropping them from her apron. Although she may appear sinister, she was actually much loved, as an ancient, abiding presence.

The face of Cailleach may be seen in grey rock and drizzle. Call her for extra strength, wits and endurance, when you need these.

Death and rebirth – a fourth aspect

Just when we may feel we have neatly encapsulated an idea, another angle shifts into perspective, reminding us that all is fluid. So, in addition to the Triple Goddess, a fourth aspect may be discerned, hard to define, mysterious, and yet suggested by the trio.

The number four suggests square groundedness. Groupings of four often indicate our earthly position, as in the four points of the compass, or in the four traditional elements of Earth, Fire, Air and Water. The Celtic cross, or quartered circle is an ancient symbol of completion, and magical rites are carried out in a circle, where the four elements have been invoked at the four cardinal points, for protection. With this in mind, it seems our fourth goddess completes the circle.

In terms of the four directions, the Maiden corresponds to

Air, East, to the dawning light of morning and to spring. The Mother is equated with the warmth of the South, Fire, midday and summer, while the Crone resides in the West, abode of sunset and autumn and the element Water. In the Northern Hemisphere, however, the North is the dark, blind side of the sky, equated with midnight, winter and the Earth element, home of the infinite stars, where Moon and Sun do not venture – and here we may meet the person of the Goddess Present and Unseen.

In a sense this fourth aspect embraces the other three, but in another she is a separate entity. While the Crone may suggest death and rebirth this goddess embodies it. She is the very person of transformation, of the intergalactic void where all life began but no life can survive. She is paradox and mystery, and she is mistress of magic. We cannot understand her, but we meet her in the dark night of the soul, when her blackness enfolds us and rebirths us into a new panorama. She is goddess of the burial mound, the tomb that is also womb, and she is our source. She is the soundless voice within that comes to us on moonless nights – listen for her, meditate upon her, and make a space in your heart for her, for her wisdom transcends all we know.

The seasons

The seasonal round can easily be related to the Triple Goddess, as we saw above, spring naturally relating to the Maiden, summer to the Mother, autumn and winter to the Crone – or, of course, winter may be related to the Unseen Goddess. However, the faces of the Goddess merge, so that we may see two, three or all countenances at once, in a landscape or seasonal celebration. For instance, at Yule the Crone is present, in the short, aged winter days. Mother, too is there, for she gives birth anew to the Sun god, and as she also rebirths herself, the

39

graceful presence of the Maiden dances in snow and frost. The Goddess Present and Unseen is there in the long, starry nights and the holy mystery of renewal. We can feel free to call up the presence of the Goddess in whatever way She inspires us, during the seasons of our lives.

The Moon

Links between lunar cycles and the Triple Goddess are self-evident and we can use observation of lunations to enable us to draw closer to the Divine Feminine in Her cyclicity and eternal presence. Lunar phases are given in calendars and diaries (see Useful Addresses), and you can check the night sky, to find the Moon.

The waxing Moon appears as a crescent in early evening, often of scintillating beauty in a still-rosy sky – this is the Maiden. In the Northern Hemisphere the waxing crescent can be cupped in a raised right hand, the reverse is true for the Southern Hemisphere. The full Moon, light of the Mother, turns the midnight to silver, while the waning crescent appears in the small hours, she is the Crone. The days of the dark Moon, when she is not seen at all, may be related to the Unseen Goddess. By her disappearance and renewal she teaches us about the abstract, about continuity, faith and rebirth.

The phases of menstruation may be linked to the Moon, and many women ovulate at full Moon and menstruate at dark Moon. With this cycle it is easy to identify with Maiden, after the period, Mother at ovulation, and Crone – when we tend to feel 'witchy' and need solitude – as the Moon wanes. The transformation 'rebirth' time of the period may relate to the mysterious Goddess aspect. Obviously if your cycle doesn't fit in so neatly, you will need to adapt, always taking the time to identify your inner feelings rather than deciding intellectually what they should be. Menstruation is discussed at length in

Chapter 5, and lunar observance, also, receives a small chapter to itself, as it is very important.

The Goddess Bride

Our look at the Triple Goddess cannot be complete without contemplating the Celtic goddess Bride – pronounced 'breed' – who is perhaps the quintessential Triple Goddess.

Bride is goddess of poetry, healing and smithcraft. She is 'the bright one' – supernal mother, bestowing creative inspiration and fertility, protectress, warrior and guardian of the young. Her role as goddess of smiths links her firmly with transformative powers, as blacksmiths, who wrought mysterious changes in metal, were considered lucky and 'magical'. Bride was known throughout the Celtic world by the various names of Brigid, Brigantia, Brigit, and she was adopted by the Christians – as were so many of the old gods and festivals – in the person of St Bridget, well known as the premier female saint of Ireland. Her sacred flame was tended at Kildare by priestesses and, subsequently, nuns. Bride is also goddess of fire.

Bride invented whistling, to call her friends. Witches were feared for their power to whistle up storms, and it is said that a whistling woman is up to no good, for whistling is a carefree, casual, cheeky activity not appropriate to modest maidens! Bride also invented the mourning sound of keening, when she lost her beloved son in the tradition of the Great Mother. She was goddess of the green earth, honoured for her fertility.

Her special feast day is Imbolc, on 2 February, which is sometimes called the Feast of the Poets. At this time, when the ground may be still hard and white with snow, or when tender snowdrops brave the keen air, the ewes' milk begins to flow at the first lambing. This is a bright festival of inspiration and creativity, when we may see the very first stirrings of spring revival, and yet remember the long, meditative nights of winter.

You may observe this festival by setting aside some time for a special creative act, from cookery to painting, and by lighting three white candles in honour of the Triple Goddess as Bride.

Practice

There have been several things with which to practise in this chapter. In addition to these you may like to reflect on the three aspects of the Goddess in turn, listing all the qualities and gifts of each and identifying where you feel you have the greatest lack. You may like to link these reflections with the appropriate lunar phase, discussed in Chapter 4. Light candles also, if you wish. White is traditional for the Maiden, red for the Mother and black for the Crone. If, however, you wish to reserve black for the fourth, mysterious face of the Goddess, then the Crone may be represented by dark blue, brown or purple. The fourth phase of the Goddess requires a different attitude – do not approach Her with thoughts and lists, but rather allow yourself to become still, so She may approach you. Contemplating all the aspects of the Goddess may awaken our appreciation of powers within ourselves that we had not formerly suspected, or valued, and can help us greatly through life's transitions.

4

the moon
goddess

. . . tender is the night
And haply the Queen-Moon is on her throne

Keats, *Ode to a Nightingale*

The Goddess smiles on us in the radiant Moon. She fills the air
with magic and her silvery touch transforms the blinding
colours of day into subtle shadows. She whispers to us of possible dreams and of other dimensions, for she is mistress of
transformation, sovereign of the Unconscious. Many goddesses
have been linked to the Moon, for by night the instinctual holds
sway – and intuition has long been a female province. We have
seen that the three lunar phases are associated with the three
stages of a woman's life, as Maiden, Mother and Crone, and

43

these phases are intimately connected to the female rhythms of menstruation and pregnancy. The gleaming egg of full Moon suggests fecundity. More than this, the Moon is the celestial embodiment of cycles that occur on Earth.

To Palaeolithic people the phases of the Moon contained a promise of renewal. As the Moon decayed, disappeared and was reborn in the new crescent, so humans could expect rebirth. There is no stronger metaphor for rebirth than the phases of the Moon. The importance of this is still appreciated by African Bushmen, probably one of the oldest races on Earth. They are described by Laurens van der Post as dancing all night, to show their love for the waning Moon, so she would return. Artefacts from the Stone Age display considerable awareness of lunar phases. For instance, the well-known 'Goddess of Willendorf' dating from about 19,000 BCE displays seven strata of notched circles on her head, and these are probably related to the seven days (approximately) of each of the lunar quarters.

The Moon appears as goddess of life and death, Lady of the tomb that is also womb. Darkness and light, death and life were revealed as complementary and mutually supportive – and all an expression of the Goddess. In most parts of the globe lunar mythology predates solar mythology by centuries. To early people the Moon was a powerful representation of the sacred, showing patterns, creating associations, epitomising both sundering and continuing. By her existence the Moon satisfied the paradox of life that demands death to continue – the survival drama of the hunt, and life that is an unending spiral, a continuum contained within the Goddess. Many ancient sacred mounds, where the dead were interred, were built facing moonrise, to the east, so the souls of the ancestors might travel along the moonbeams.

The Moon – gifts and associations

As humankind graduated from the hunter-gatherer stage into an agrarian community, links were observed between the lunar cycle and that of the seed. The Moon swells from nothingness, growing through a slender sickle into the full, blooming orb, in much the same way that the seed lies dormant in the darkness underground, puts forth shoots and grows to a flourishing plant. Then follows the cycle of decay. The waning crescent is swallowed in the sky, as the plant turns to seed and reduces once more to the soil. The invisible time of transformation and gestation follows. Great and incomprehensible events occur in secrecy, until the tiny shoot once more appears, the Moon's sliver rises in the evening sky.

Lunar cycle also epitomises completion and balance, for the phases can be represented in a circle, quartered in the shape of the Celtic cross – this is a simple mandala, meaning wholeness, and has important psychological associations for our own centre of balance, the Self. So, going clockwise, dark Moon appears

opposite full Moon, waxing opposite waning, and the cycle appears in its entirety. Such circular motifs are employed in rituals, because their effect on the Unconscious is potent – the circle means eternity, protection and concentration of power, plus many more things. The four phases, dark, waxing, full and waning may then be linked to the four traditional elements that compose our world – Earth, Air, Fire, and Water, relating also, respectively to North, East, South, and West, the quarters that define our space.

Extending from this, we may plot the seasons, as marked by the ancient festivals, around the circle. Yule, the Midwinter Solstice, corresponds with North/Earth/dark Moon, Spring Equinox to East/Air/waxing Moon, Midsummer Solstice to South/Fire/full Moon and Autumn Equinox to West/Water/waning Moon. The cross-quarter festivals are then plotted in between, with Imbolc and Beltane during the waxing part of the cycle, and Lammas and Samhain during the waning. Readers in the Southern Hemisphere may prefer to rotate these associations through 180 degrees, associating dark Moon, Earth, etc. with South, for the 'blind' side of the sky where Sun and Moon never appear is traditionally related to the element Earth. In addition, it may be more appropriate to plot the cycle anti-clockwise for the Southern Hemisphere, as Moon, Sun and all the heavens are there seen to move this way.

The gifts of the Moon to humanity were faith, an understanding of cycle and an acceptance of the mysteries of transformation and rebirth. From the disappearance and reappearance of the Moon we may have learnt to think in the abstract, becoming able to hold an idea in our heads even while the object had disappeared. The Moon is an ever-present reminder of cyclicity and an embodiment of mystery. If we rationalise the light of the Moon and her phases in terms of astronomy, we lose the sacred perspective upon life, we forget that life is a metaphor for spirit, and we distance ourselves from our immanent Goddess.

Lunar effects

As Queen of the Night, the Moon is related to the Unconscious, to the irrational patterns of response that underpin our lives, to the tides of dreams and emotions and memory. These tides have their own laws. They link us to the universal and we ignore them to our detriment. Because of her relationship with the seas the Moon is further linked to the womb of all life, the primordial ocean. We, whose bodies are largely water, respond to the Moon, although we may not realise it. It is well documented that full Moon marks a rise in crime, accidents and entry to lunatic asylums – the word 'lunatic' derives from 'luna' meaning moon. Haemorrhage on the operating table is more likely at full Moon. The energies now abroad are unsettling to a 'rational' consciousness.

Much weather and gardening lore exists in regard to the Moon, and often there will be a weather change at new or full Moon. Seeds planted when the Moon is waxing germinate faster, and most pruning and harvesting is best undertaken with a waning Moon. Planning our activities in relation to lunar phases can give a sense of deep satisfaction and harmony with Nature. More than this, the lunar phases can be celebrated, with veneration and enchantment, as they have been in secret grove, temple and star-crested hill, from ancient times.

Lunar festivals

There is no better and more immediate way to make contact with our Goddess than by celebrating the phases of the Moon. This can be done quite informally – for instance, full Moon is a good time to have friends to supper or throw a party, and if all are Moon worshippers so much the better. Quiet observances can take the form of moonlit walks and meditation. You may like to celebrate with a bottle of wine or special biscuits in the

47

shape of a crescent. Lighting a candle is a simple, ritual act. You may like to refer back to our Practice session at the end of Chapter 3 and link this with lunar phases.

Lunar phases have been festive occasions since prehistory. Present-day pagans and Goddess worshippers often celebrate full Moon at a festival called an 'Esbat'. During this the presence of the Goddess may be drawn down upon a priestess in a stirring invocation. This is called 'The Great Mother Charge' and has been rewritten from earlier material by a priestess of our century, Doreen Valiente. Because it is so expressive it is here quoted in its entirety. The priestess speaks:

> *Whenever ye have need of anything, once in a month, better it be when the Moon is full, then shall ye gather together in some secret place and adore the spirit of me, who am Queen of all witches. There shall ye assemble; ye who would fain learn all sorcery yet have not yet won its deepest secrets. To thee will I teach things as yet unknown. And ye shall be free from slavery, and as a sign that ye be truly free ye shall be naked in your rites; and ye shall sing, dance, feast, make music and love all in my praise. For mine is the ecstasy of the spirit and mine also is joy on Earth, for my law is love unto all beings. Keep pure your highest ideal, strive ever towards it, let none stop you or turn you aside. For mine is the secret door which opens upon the Land of Youth, and mine is the cup of the wine of life, and the Cauldron of Cerridwen, which is the Holy Grail of immortality. I am the gracious Goddess who gives the gift of joy unto the heart of man. Upon Earth I give the knowledge of the spirit eternal; beyond death I give peace, freedom and reunion with those who have gone before. Nor do I demand sacrifice, for behold, I am the Mother of all living, and my love is poured out upon the Earth.*

The priest says:

> *Hear ye the words of the Star Goddess; She in the dust of whose feet are the hosts of heaven, and whose body encircles the Universe.*

The priestess continues:

> *I, who am the beauty of the green earth, and the white Moon among the stars and the mystery of the waters, and the desire of the heart of man call unto thy soul; Arise, and come unto me, for I am the soul of Nature, who gives life to the universe. From me all things proceed and unto me all things must return; and before my face, beloved of gods and men, let thine innermost divine self be enfolded in the rapture of the infinite. Let my worship be within the heart that rejoiceth; for behold, all acts of love and pleasure are my rituals. And therefore let there be beauty and strength, power and compassion, honour and humility, mirth and reverence within you. And thou who thinkest to seek for me, know thy seeking and yearning shall avail thee not unless thou knowest the mystery; that if that which thou seekest thou findest not within thee, thou wilt never find it without thee. For behold, I have been with thee from the beginning and I am that which is attained at the end of desire.*

The above is a beautiful and complete statement of worship of the Goddess. You may like to read this through, when the full Moon rides high, at midnight.

Man and the Moon

Although the Moon, by virtue of her associations, seems most feminine, there have been many Moon gods. Maori lore holds that the Moon is the true husband of all women, while the Papuans believe that periods are caused by intercourse with the Moon. One of the most common images perceived is that of a 'man in the Moon' and there are many tales, from various cultures, explaining how he got there. Most of these are punitive, for instance one 'moon man' is Judas, exiled for his betrayal of Jesus. These have a later, patriarchal ring, missing the point of Moon as teacher of the Mysteries. However, the Moon can be invaluable to men. Lacking the cyclicity, the intimate body knowledge and instinctual connectedness that menstruation gives women, men can learn from the Moon to experience ebb and flow and to appreciate their own inner tides.

The Jungian idea of 'anima' is well known. This is the 'inner woman' within all men, picture of his deepest desires, inspiratrice, creative flame. This often becomes fastened on to real-life women who cannot fully embody this inner goddess image, so resulting in disappointment and broken relationships. However, the anima may achieve a more useful embodiment for a man who studies the Moon as celestial Feminine, enhancing his creative powers, as well as his understanding and sensitivity. It can be a good idea for men to take note of their bodily patterns in relation to the Moon – energy, sexuality, dreams – for in this way some idea of personal rhythm can be discovered. Also, by giving your unconscious the message that moonlight, cycle and the Feminine are important, so subtly, benefits can start to appear.

Moon goddesses and myths

Selene

Because the Moon is so feminine, many goddesses can be linked to her. A Greek myth tells of the love of the Moon goddess Selene, for the handsome shepherd Endymion, whom she spotted asleep on the hillside as she rose in the sky. So irresistible did she find him that she left her gleaming chariot and came down to lie with him. But Selene grew fearful that Endymion's love might be stolen from her by a mortal woman who could be his wife. So she kissed him into eternal sleep.

At the dark of the Moon Selene is absent, because she is with her lover. However, he brings her no joy, only tears. Seeking to stop others from enjoying him she has deprived herself of his company. And so Endymion's story tells us that to benefit from the wonders and wisdom of the lunar dreamscape we must be able to return, to bring our dreams to life. It also has something to say about relationships. How many of us seek to change our loved ones, hanging on to them at any price, and then finding that what we have is a shadow of the one we love and not what we really wanted at all? In so doing we have learnt only half of the Moon's message. We must also have faith and accept letting go, as the waning Moon, and so understand the totality.

Coatlicue

The ancient Mexican goddess, Coatlicue, was originally an Earth goddess, associated with the serpent. Regularly rebirthing itself by shedding its skin, the serpent has always been associated with rebirth, the Moon and wisdom. Coatlicue went to Snake Hill to meditate, and gather white feathers to adorn herself. Remaining yet a virgin, she still became miraculously pregnant and gave birth to Quetzalcoatl, the feathered serpent, sacrificial saviour-god.

Coatlicue existed before all else, drifting in the mists of time-before-time. The Sun and his mages did not at first realise her importance, but when they did they brought her gifts and charms to show their love, and she shone forth as mother of the cosmos. She was called a Moon divinity, wife to the Sun. However, Coatlicue was also death mother, honoured with spring flowers, yet often depicted wearing skulls, claws and a skirt of serpents, and so she is the devouring spirit of the dark Moon as well as Full Moon Lady.

Practice

If you wish to develop a habit of honouring the Goddess, lunar phases give you the best opportunity. Start by noting full and dark Moons on your calendar or diary. Plan to celebrate in a way that seems best – some suggestions have been given in this chapter. Anything you do should fit in with your lifestyle and commitments. Simply opening the curtains to let the Moon shine in can be an act of worship.

You may like to set aside a small corner or shelf to make a Goddess altar, and you may feature the Moon's phases on this. Place stones such as rose quartz, pearl, moonstone and aquamarine. Perhaps silver artefacts, shells, animal or goddess figures. You may like to place different goddess figures on your altar to mark the different phases. Maiden goddesses like Artemis may look youthful and energetic for the waxing phase. Isis or Demeter for maternal full Moon and Crone images such as Hecate or Cailleach as the Moon wanes. At dark Moon you could choose to drape an image with black cloth, to signify the Goddess Present and Unseen or you may feel she is expressed by a figure like Hecate anyway. Go with what evokes the most appropriate response in you. Cards and calendars, designed by Jane Brideson, the illustrator of this book, can also be obtained, depicting the phases of the Moon, and these are available from a source given at the back of the book. Marking the Moon's phases, in whatever way you choose, can add another dimension to your life.

5

menstruation – red moon mysteries

. . . The window must be shut, cacophony held at bay
while I repair my raveled senses.
The miracle of blood demands this, reminding me . . .
of ancient stillness in the leafy glade, solitude and the moon . . .

Sherri Rose-Walker, *Ancient Stillness*

The Goddess is woman, divine and complete, embodying all aspects of femininity in holy, full-blooded glory. And so, naturally, the Goddess menstruates. We see this in the lunar phases, where either dark or full Moon may be taken as the

menstrual time. In this chapter we shall consider the importance of menstruation as a cultural and personal force, how it
contains the essence of feminine power, and how observing its
rhythms can bring us closer to the Divine, internally and
externally.

Prevailing attitudes

Even today taboos persist regarding menstruation, and we need
to consider this first. Even the most open-minded of us may
have inhibitions and preconceptions, hardly conscious though
these may be, and these must be dismantled before we can
truly explore the magic and meanings of menstruation.

At the time of writing, in the mid-1990s, the advertising of
sanitary protection has only fairly recently appeared on our tele-
vision screens. Toilet paper, on the other hand, has long been
presented with cute whimsy. Sanitary protection, usually
changed in the bathroom and used by half the population for a
great part of their adult life, has been a subject for discreet
whispers. Now we have sanitary towels and their virtues dis-
played – but the liquid they are seen to absorb so efficiently is
a clinical blue. Yet menstrual blood is not excrement. It is the
colour of wine, has little odour, and is the testament to each
woman's sacrifice, creativity and power. It is the flower of her
sexuality – the pun is intentional! It is hard to see why menstruation has been such a matter for concealment.

Young girls still despise their periods, calling them 'yukky',
plugging them with tampons and resenting their interference in
activities, studies, work and social life, that are all planned in
linear time, never considering that it may be the routines that
are at fault, not the period, and that perhaps different rhythms
– rhythms played out by women – might be more suitable than
the dry strictures of a timetable. Women insult the symphonies
of their bodies by calling periods 'the curse'. Who was cursed,

and why? Eve, of course, for challenging patriarchal authority. Men's attitudes range through disgust, avoidance, embarrassment, irritation, patronisation, sympathy and drug prescription. Hormones are administered, wombs are removed, as if the whole business was some kind of aberration, which to masculine consciousness it may indeed seem. Respect, appreciation, fascination, awe at this creation of Nature – all these are missing, and conspicuously so among women themselves, who rarely consider that their pain and distress may be due to the fact that the cycle is continually being fought, like a swimmer struggling upstream. Periods have long been a source of shame. To women competing head to head with men in today's world, they are a nuisance, at best.

Things would be very different if men menstruated. There would be cults, clubs, societies created to approach this manifestation in different ways. Scientific research would be intense. Working life and recreation would revolve around this all-important bleeding. Indeed, it is hard to imagine the endless debates, the fathomless interest, the extent to which the function would be exalted! Why has the female period been a matter of concealment, unease, distaste? Could it be because it is a source of power?

If women marginalise, ignore or despise their periods they are doing themselves a great disservice, and yet very many of us do. Now it is usual to discuss openly such things as PMS and sanitary protection, but still the sense of shame, nuisance, uncleanliness and unpleasantness pervades. We don't consider our periods a gift, a divine cadence, the ebb and flow of hormones providing us with limitless experience of different levels of consciousness, of creative inspiration. We are not allowed to value – or indeed to have – meditative seclusion at the time of the period. We do not see menstrual blood as beautiful, proof of our depth and wisdom as women. We do not value the fact that we may feel completely different at different times of the month, that we have access to more than one aspect of self-expression. We seek to iron out the cycle, clear up the mess, and this attitude is so general that most of us have no inkling to what enormous extent we are 'selling out' to male-dominated attitudes that have pervaded for centuries, and how we are amputating a great part of our abilities and potentialities as women and human beings.

At this time when the Goddess is re-emerging, it is also time to consider deeply and at length just to what extent menstruation has been ignored and devalued. Perhaps our attitudes need to be adjusted.

Tradition and Lore

Taboos and tribal lore on menstruation abound. In Leviticus rules are given about uncleanliness concerning menstrual blood. Sex at the time of the period meant drawing close to Lilith, Adam's first, dark bride – more of Lilith later. The Dogon tribe in Africa segregate menstruating females to a special hut, and they are not alone in this custom. The origin of this, however, is likely to be the recognition of female power as shamans and seers at this time, rather than the subsequent attribution of 'uncleanliness'. Women of our own culture might imagine the glee with which these women retire to their seclusion, away from the relentless everyday demands! Pliny writes of the evil characteristics of the menstruating individual. Even today such activities as swimming and sex, both of which may be very desirable at the time of the period, are still often proscribed.

Secret desire and fascination for blood is revealed in vampire lore, even in such films as *The Exorcist* we are given much symbolism connected with repression of the rising energies of the menarche, which is turned into a terrifying and destructive demon. Most cultures contain a myth that in some time-before-time men stole wisdom and power from women, and while menstruation may be very much feared, it is also imitated by men. Circumcision at puberty may be a way to emulate the natural blood shed by women. The horrible rite of slitting the penis to resemble a bleeding vagina, called subincision, has similar significance, though much more extreme. An Aboriginal native, quoted by Shuttle and Redgrove, in *The Wise Wound* speaks of men's circumcision rites: 'We have been stealing what belongs to them (women) . . . Men have nothing to do really, except copulate . . .'

It is worth noting that cultures where menstruation and all its attendant meanings have been repressed are the most aggressive and bloody – where the wise and gentle blood is not valued, is driven into the Unconscious, there we have blood of death and destruction. Our own civilisation is a prime example! By contrast, Jamie Sams, in *The 13 Original Clan Mothers* (see Further Reading) speaks of the White Buffalo Tradition of women's Healing Quest at their moontimes. Women do not need to undertake the gruelling vision quests more common among males. Jamie Sams tells us 'The Great Mystery does not ask further suffering or pain of any woman. Womankind is already doing her part by giving birth to children, as well as giving birth to the dreams of humankind . . .' Each period, or important lunar phase, for those who have had a hysterectomy or the menopause, is a time of special, quiet retreat and healing.

Fear of menstruation can be detected in witch hunts, where the idea of the 'witch' woman gave rise to paranoia, the like of which has rarely been recorded. Women, in their menstrual cycle, possess the transformative abilities of the witch. Masculine, left-brain consciousness, however, has a terror of any feminine power except that of procreating a dynasty – bearing the father's name, of course. The time when a woman is least likely to conceive, when she is likely to overthrow accepted cultural values, when she may be inspired, rebellious, different, may be seen as very threatening, and so the blood becomes linked to the cannibalisation of babies, the destruction of family values, common decency and all that is wholesome.

These ideas may seem strange to you if you are used to thinking about periods in the culturally accepted manner. They are explored at length in *The Wise Wound* (see Further Reading). If you accept the idea that periods are a messy nuisance, perhaps you could begin to think about all the implications, even if they seem far fetched at first. Isn't there a special 'aura' to the whole subject – and isn't that ambience connected to unease, even fear? We have a saying: 'Where there's fear, there's power'.

Periods and the Moon

The average female cycle spans about twenty-eight or twenty-nine days. The passage of the Moon, from new, through waxing, full and waning, back to new again, takes twenty-nine and a half days. The connection between these cycles is most significant. Lunar cycles suggest transformation and rebirth. They lend themselves to a cyclic, spiralling concept of time, as opposed to a linear one. Early calendars were based on the Moon and many words are derived from this fact – menstruation, month, commensurate, etc. In a sense the Moon demonstrates and symbolises the menstruation of the Goddess, Her cyclicity and Her ability to change from one aspect to another.

The Moon has long been linked to the instinctual senses. When the Sun goes down and the Moon comes up, perspectives alter, shadows deepen, and a candle flame, invisible by bright sunlight, dances like a demon for the Moon. It is not only the human female cycle that is affected by the Moon. Animals' sexual activity is at its height at full Moon. Herrings and eels swarm, insects are affected by the cycle. The Moon, goddess of the tides, is goddess of the watery womb, and the primeval sea which was the source of all life.

The attunement women have with the Moon-cycle is evidence of their links with the forces of Nature, the pulse of the Goddess, and suggests that periods are a key to intuitive wisdom. Many women menstruate at new Moon and ovulate at full Moon, when the Moon hangs in the sky like a great, glistening egg. Other women menstruate at full Moon and ovulate at dark Moon, and this has been called the 'wise woman' cycle, for there are suggestions that it may link with creativity, while ovulating at full Moon links more with mothering physical children. The light of the full Moon can stimulate ovulation in women who are having problems in this area.

There are also women who do not menstruate at these times, and who may have a cycle other than the classic twenty-nine day rhythm. However, studies suggest that these may still find that lunar rhythms are affecting them in more subtle ways – for instance, a longer cycle may link with new Moon one month and the full Moon that follows six weeks later. Only by taking careful note can a woman plot the links between her own cycle and that of the Moon. It seems that women who have taken careful note of their menstrual cycle, and who have worked with it and learnt from it, experience far less trouble at the menopause. It may be that if you have already had the menopause, all is not over. By attuning to lunar cycle, by watching the ebb and flow of emotion, dream, sensation, activity in yourself, in response to these rhythms, it may be possible to recreate the very same cycle of wisdom as offered by the monthly period.

Shaping our culture

It seems very likely that the adoption by females of a menstrual cycle as opposed to an oestrus cycle has been crucial in the formation of society as we know it. In humans sexual desire and receptiveness is not linked merely to procreation, but it is continuous. Thus, because of the monthly period, lasting partnerships with a whole spectrum of sexual behaviour have become possible. Menstruation, then, can be seen as the greatest gift of the Love Goddess, encouraging humans to explore the pleasures and possibilities of erotic relationship at every nuance of the cycle – and eroticism can, of course, be mental, spiritual, emotional, as well as physical. With this in mind, it is a great shame to neglect the different, enhancing gifts of the period.

In addition, of course, menstruation has meant that women do sometimes say 'No' when they might be expected to say 'Yes'. Animals on heat do not deny sex to any male that arrives. Human females, on the other hand, are much more complex. To please them, to find ways of relating and understanding on many levels is likely to be the requirement for any male who wishes to get close, sexually. And so humans have learnt the talent of sensitivity and true communication through the period – the women learnt it from the Moon and communicated it to the men. Z. Budapest in *Grandmother Moon* (see Further Reading) writes: 'What women did with their bodies liberated our species from the incessant burden of breeding and separated the idea of sex from procreation. Sex became a separate cultural factor, for pleasure and enjoyment, for romance and love affairs. Procreation became a choice for women, a choice won millenia ago.' Sadly, as we know, men can become angry at women who say 'No'. They may become aggressive and coercive. We can see in thousands of ways how men have been unwilling to learn about things 'feminine' in the narrowest and the broadest senses, and how destructive our society has become, as a result.

The power and poetry of the period

So what is the magic of the swirl of hormones that constitutes the period, the double spiral of the womb and ovary, oestrogen and progesterone, ovulation and menstruation? What is the inner meaning of the mood swings and the symptoms, and how can our periods enhance our Goddess consciousness?

The menstrual cycle is unseen, the saga of the egg unsung, but we must remember that this takes place in the cradle of life – womb and ovary, where we all began, and it is *much* more than just a stomach ache. A woman's cycle radically affects her life and that of her nearest and dearest, infiltrating the dreams of partner and children and affecting their moods, also. When I am premenstrual my sons have tantrums and accidents, that may well draw blood. At the start of my period once, my husband had a fearful dream to do with black fruit, and awoke saying 'We mustn't have black cherries'. Being – I hope – wiser, my symbolic answer was to go out and buy black cherries, for the mysteries of the period, of the dark time of ending and new beginnings, were just what we did want, and what he needed to accept. The point here is that different elements may emerge from consciousness, new perspectives, values of the inward, the transformative, and the woman with her greater body wisdom can mediate these if she has the confidence, the acceptance. Accidents and bad moods are resistance to this, but it is not hard to see that the woman may be blamed for all of this, called 'witchy' and persecuted. Thereby vast continents of wisdom have been relegated to the shadowlands.

Many myths tell of the descent of a hera/hero to an Underworld, where initiation struggles must be faced before re-ascent can be achieved. The goddess Inanna and Persephone come to mind, as does Christ's descent to hell. These are metaphors for the crossing of the initiation threshold towards menstruation. A physical child is not going to arrive. Energies turn towards the magical child, the right-brain, instinctual consciousness, the part that demands self-expression, not devotion to procreation and home-building. The bleeding time is shamanic, when mystical communion with the body and the inner 'wise wound' make possible transition to other levels of consciousness. Traditionally shamans are 'wounded' in some way, and this wound serves as an opening to other dimensions. However, every woman is wounded, internally, at her period. The energies of power animals may become available, and the animus, or inner man may appear in his dark guise as the magician, or Horned God, helping the woman by his presence in dreams. This is the radical time that may appear destructive to family values, and so may be strongly resisted by 'motherly' women, and men generally, so giving rise to severe PMS. There is a secret guilt, and sorrow that the egg has 'died'.

The drama of the egg may be the guiding vision behind adventurous tales of hazardous journeys and heroic acts. Each month the 'chosen' egg makes it way to the surface of the ovary, takes sail down the fallopian tube to the uncharted uterine sea. There the Beloved may be found – a fertilising sperm – and safe berth (birth?) achieved in the womb wall. Or the egg may, as usually happens, be swept out into the dark dreamworld of non-being. In a sense this is the metaphor for many creative ideas – possibly to be fleshed out, incubated and taking form in a creation, or, more likely, slipping back into the unconscious pool. It is a tale of potential, of passage into and out of manifestation, of transformation. It is also a tale of the egg-ego's bid to survive, not to be swept away on the shoreless sea of unconsciousness. The 'inner man' at this time may appear in dreams as a fatherly, protective figure, who turns to stern judge and persecutor, as it becomes obvious fertilisation will not take place. As the egg is expelled a woman may dream of being tried and burnt as a witch.

It is little wonder that masculine consciousness, with its left-brain orientation and greater sense of ego, should value the ovulation process, when creation of a tangible child may take place, and the threat of deeper meanings avoided. Many women concur with this perspective, but more 'divergent' women – artists, activists, witches – value the menstrual pole of experience most highly, and may experience a pre-ovulation syndrome as egg tension mounts.

Union of opposites

Menstruation offers women the opportunity to make conscious unaccessed areas of the psyche. At ovulation left-brain logic is supreme, while during menstruation the instinctual right brain reigns. Crossing the thresholds between these are powerful initiations. Most women will favour one end of the experience, menstruation or ovulation, more highly than the other, according to whether their tendency is to conform (motherly, dynastic, ovulatory) or to diverge (artistic, individual, menstrual). However, the goal is that the poles of experience both receive respect and are made conscious, valued. Vivid dreams adumbrate and enliven the process, aiding passage – dreams should be carefully logged in connection with the cycle, as these are the language of the unconscious mind. Women have a better connection between their two brain hemispheres than men, and they can communicate the greater levels of response, sympathy and enlightenment. In this, menstruation can be the key to efficient dialogue between the ego and the Unconscious, between the logical and the mystical, between the subjective and the objective. It is hardly an exaggeration to say that this is just what the planet needs. We have to retain the benefits of the scientific approach while retrieving the sense of oneness with the Divine and with Nature, that may well be our only salvation, at a time when science and consumerism are devouring our environment. Conscious following of the menstrual pattern, creating dialogue between the two poles of menstruation and ovulation and the drastically differing experiences these represent, may be the only way of achieving harmony and growth in consciousness.

Observation of menstruation may be also the path to

transcendent sex, respecting as it does the delicate, mutable and powerful female responses. In this, women show men the way. The entire cycle is one that a man can follow, with his partner, matching his dreams to hers and learning to deepen his own experiences by identifying with her, so enhancing his own pleasure and depth of feeling. There are things that men may be able to experience only through a female, because their connection with their bodies, with rhythm and source, is comparatively tenuous. And good sex – really good sex, which trembles on the threshold of the mystical and sometimes plunges over it – is a pathway to the Goddess. As put by Shuttle and Redgrove: 'What God or demon separated religion and sexuality, the highest aspiration of people from their greatest sympathetic capabilities?' (*Alchemy for Women* – see Further Reading). Goddess worship shows us clearly that the gifts of the body are certainly the way to the Divine. In this, as in so many things, women can lead – and lead does not mean dominate. It means that she who carries the lamp goes first.

Myths and goddesses

Lilith

Lilith was the first wife of Adam, and her name is derived from the Sumerian Queen of Heaven, Lil, meaning air, or storm – the dark, wild side of Inanna. The name Lilith is also connected to 'owl' – the sinister bird of prey that swoops, soundless in the darkness, and yet is symbolic of all wisdom. Hebrew myth tells how Lilith was fashioned from soiled earth, and yet we all know of the richness and potential of compost! So Lilith, though unclean, was in a sense equal, for she was made separately from Adam, while his subsequent wife, Eve, was fashioned from a rib. Lilith refuses to submit to Adam's authority and she flies from him, to give birth to hordes of demons. It was Lilith whom medieval men feared, coming to them in dreams to suck forth their semen, and Lilith was also feared as devourer of children. She embodies free, sexual and feral feminine energy, women's desires that are individual, uncluttered by cultural and family requirements. She is the wild woman, true to herself and no other, conforming to no expectations, following her instincts with the splendour of a lioness, the stealth of a bat. She is what all men desire and what most fear – and she is who all women are, in their heart of hearts, especially at the period.

So Lilith is the menstrual spirit that demands to find its own resting place, in blasted tree, cave, hillside or in studio, study, garden and kitchen. She is supremely creative because her inspiration is pure, undiluted by anyone's expectations. She is vivid and beautiful, she is the spice of life, and she is only dangerous when thwarted by those who value solely physical children, who see her as a murderess and who do not value her unique gifts. One of the gifts of Lilith is sexual experience that rends mind and body, opening a pathway to Underworld mysterious treasures – sex at the period, when conception is most unlikely. As you menstruate, open your window to the night wind, and invite Lilith in.

Sekhmet

Sekhmet was the Egyptian, lion-headed Sun-goddess, whose mane flamed like solar flares. With Sekhmet the Goddess comes into her full power, searing, blinding. These solar-type energies may be felt most when the Sun is in conjunction with the Moon, in the same astrological sign, and this is the time of the dark-of-the-Moon, when she is not visible. And so, the dark goddess time is also the burning goddess time – and dark Moon is when many women menstruate. The lion, as a power animal, is about queendom, fierce self-possession, predatory – and yet protective.

Although we have emphasised the Moon, there have also been many solar goddesses, and Sekhmet is one of the most brilliant and awesome. Myth tells how she became bloodthirsty, and slaughtered thousand upon thousands of humans. It seemed her blood-lust could not be slaked, and the gods became worried that she would leave no worshippers alive. So 7,000 jars of beer were brewed and mixed with red powder, to resemble blood – the number seven is interesting, with its lunar connections. As the morning Sun rose the goddess saw her reflection in the beer, drank it and retired, drunk, to her palace. And so humanity was saved.

Sekhmet's blood-lust tells of the strong, instinctual desire to experience the internal wound, to see the menstrual blood and to make the transition to the menstrual experience, where the thirst for self-knowledge has a hope of being satisfied. Sekhmet sees her reflection – she is no vampire on a graveyard quest, but she finds regeneration, as all women can at their period. The energies of the period – as with Lilith – are only destructive if frustrated. We can appease Sekhmet with our blood as she pads, snarling into our lives, and partake of her power and her fierceness. I suspect the myth has been given a patriarchal slant. Sekhmet is not to be deceived by beer, but through surrender to her, opening our senses to all meanings, we can achieve menstrual reverie akin to intoxication and find our true power as females. At menstruation, snuggle into bed, stroke your sore tummy, and listen to Sekhmet purr.

Maiden, Mother and Crone

The Triple Goddess and the Moon have been discussed earlier. During the menstrual cycle a woman can be seen to pass through all of the aspects. After menstruation she is in a sense 'rebirthed' and may feel 'maidenish'. At ovulation she is 'mother' with all the receptive, nurturing characteristics, while as her period approaches she is crone-like as her vision turns inward. At the period perhaps a woman's fourth, transformative aspect feels closer. If the period occurs at dark Moon the connection may be even more obvious. Remembering this can be revealing for women observing their cycle.

Practice

If you have found some of this chapter rather strange and new, an important 'practice' will be to reflect upon it, and see if your perspectives begin to alter. There is much to practise with this chapter. Let us begin with practical matters.

Sanitary protection

Most available sanitary protection is friendly neither to the environment nor to women's bodies. The bleach and fibres of tampons may cause irritation, and in extreme cases their use has caused toxic shock and even death. Sanitary towels pollute the seas and wash up on beaches. What might we do instead?

Menstrual sponges are an alternative to tampons. For these you need to buy a *natural* sponge, and cut it to the required size. One natural sponge will be enough to supply you with several menstrual sponges, so you can experiment, carefully. The size that is suitable for you will depend on the size of your insides and whether or not you are a virgin, have had children, etc. Be careful here. Even though I have had three children, the most comfortable size for me is still only about 6–8 cms in length, 2–3 cm in diameter. You can use different sizes at different stages of your period, with bigger ones obviously better on heavy days.

To insert the sponge you will need to wet it, squeeze out most of the water and push it in. This can feel somewhat uncomfortable. After a while you may feel the sponge has started to leak, but initially this will just be the remaining water, coming out first. When you need to remove the sponge, do so carefully, for the sponge will feel like you, and you don't want to damage your insides. It is always possible to extract the sponge, but very young women may panic. If you have just started your periods you will need the help of an older woman as you get to know your body. Don't push the sponge up too far, and use only a very small one at first. If you are a virgin, inserting the sponge may feel painful to the point of impossibility! Don't worry, there's nothing wrong with you. It just means the vagina needs gentle stretching and a sponge may not suit you at this time.

A saturated sponge needs to be rinsed thoroughly before re-insertion, so this can be an awkward method if your period is heavy and you are away from home. For medium to light days, however, it can be great. Give yourself a few months to get used to sponges, for they are strange at first. Never wash your sponge in soap powder or detergent – just use plain water and allow the sponge to dry naturally if you aren't reusing it immediately.

You may also make washable cloth pads from thick towels or nappies, but these are more difficult to use, and may be inconvenient for some lifestyles. Nonetheless, if you are able to stay at home, they are the best way to deal with a heavy day. Alternatively, reusable proprietory brands are available (see Useful Addresses). This isn't a step back to the Dark Ages, but a way forward, to respecting the cycle and caring for your feminine body.

Adjusting your routine

Routines are geared to men's linear perception of time, not women's cyclical activity, and it might suit many women far better to have five-day breaks every month, working more intensively at other times. If you are able to adjust your activities to your cycle, then do so. If you feel languorous at your period then sit or lie, walk, sway to music and let yourself dream. If your dreams inspire you, you will be able to use these inspirations later, but now just let them flow, taking notes or speaking into a cassette-recorder if you like. But even doing nothing is beneficial, for this time has value in itself.

If you are tied to routine in your job, then give yourself early nights, late mornings, if you can. Allow yourself to do what you wish, as far as possible, and don't force yourself into a straight-jacket of someone else's making. Of course you are not ill or dysfunctional at your period, but your needs are different. Things may be moving into consciousness. You may need more space. If you can give yourself this, your effectuality at other times is likely to be greatly increased.

Sex

Sex at the period may be very special and may relieve cramps. Far from avoiding sex, you may enjoy it especially now, but differently from other times. Desire for sex tends to be intense at ovulation, but an even deeper intensity may be felt at menstruation, when a woman's approach may be more assertive, or inspired by profounder levels.

Dreams

It is of primary importance to chart your dreams, as these may be a key to the meanings of the cycle, and may give you many clues as to what you need to do and experience. Noting dreams can make the whole of life more colourful and add unseen dimensions. Merely noting the dreams, without attempting heavy interpretation, can aid transformations through ovulation/menstruation, rational/instinctual for example, and dreams can show you which stage of your cycle is currently with you. For instance, it is common to dream of eggs, pearls or jewellery at ovulation, while dreams during menstruation may feature red flowers and animals. After charting your dreams for a while, you will become alive to their personal meanings for you.

Relaxation and related matters

Learning to relax is an art, and many books are available on the subject. Some methods are briefly given in *Witchcraft – A Mobius Guide* and *Wheel of the Year* both published by Hodder and Stoughton. Regular relaxation will help greatly with periods, and massage, aromatherapy, herbal remedies, homoeopathy and acupuncture are all helpful for menstrual problems. Clary sage is an oil that is often found to soothe premenstrual tension, and it should be dissolved in a carrier oil (sweet almond or grapeseed for instance) 2 drops to 5 ml (1 teaspoon). Massage the mixture on to your abdomen or back to release tensions.

Menstrual mandala

A mandala is a circular design, a symbol of wholeness, and the menstrual cycle lends itself to portrayal in this balanced and beautiful manner. Contemplating the mandala may lead to a greater feeling of completeness, and to an understanding of how the different parts of your cycle complement each other.

To make a simple mandala, draw a large circle and

quarter it. Then divide each section into seven, so accounting for twenty-eight days. Divide each section into sub-sections, to take note of dreams (just a word or two – complex accounts can be kept in your dream-diary), feelings, aches and pains, exhilaration, sexuality, mental sharpness, etc. Note also lunar phases and the weather. You may start at the top, with day one of your period, and work around in a clockwise direction. You will need to experiment with this to find what works best for you. If your cycle is irregular you may need to continue around, outside your mandala, in a spiral.

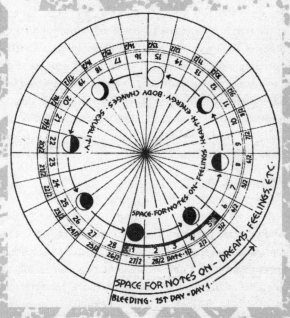

This is a sample month. The lunar phases will occur at different dates for each month.

Often noting and appreciating the cycle serves to regulate it. If your cycle spans 29 days, which is very common, connecting with the moon, then the exact four-fold division will not be right for you. Experiment with colours and designs. In the end you will have a picture of your cycle that is special to you.

C.G. Jung, the well-known psychotherapist and philosophic thinker, had much to say about the value of the mandala as a symbol for psychic wholeness. He also spoke of integrating the repressed side of the personality, or 'shadow', and of the four functions of consciousness – thinking, feeling, sensation and intuition. All these ideas are applicable to a woman's monthly experience, for each of the four functions may figure more strongly at different times of the cycle, the least conscious 'inferior' function operating most at the period. Also, Jung's concept of the 'inner man' or 'animus' is active in different ways and with different faces throughout the cycle, especially in dreams. It is not possible to cover all these areas in detail here, and I suggest further reading on this subject and list some books in 'Further Reading'.

Respecting the cycle

The best practice of all is to respect your cycle, love your body in all its manifestations and go with your feelings where at all possible. The cycle need not be fought, repressed or despised; it is not there to make your life, or anyone else's life, a misery. Menstruating women play out the descent and return of the Goddess and travel through Her forms in the monthly round. Feminine experience is rich and varied – myth come to life. And menstruation is life-enhancing, so go with the flow!

6

the descent
of the goddess

*And the peaks of the mountains and the depths of the sea echoed
with her immortal voice, and her queenly mother heard her. A
sharp pain seized her heart. With her lovely hands she tore the veil
from her long ambrosial hair . . .*

Homeric, *Hymn to Demeter*

Many myths tell of goddesses taken down into the Underworld.
These myths can teach us much. Let us look at two well-known
myths and seek to uncover some of the meanings.

Demeter and Persephone

In our Chapter 3 on the Triple Goddess we looked at the story of

Demeter as Mother Goddess. Her daughter Persephone, while out amusing herself with her friends, spots a luscious and exotic flower and decides that she must pick it. Despite the warnings of her maidens who tell her an unknown plant may be very poisonous and the ground near it looks unsafe, Persephone is determined to have the bloom. She tiptoes up to it, gingerly, and begins to pull. Harder and harder she tugs, but the stem is very strong and the roots, in fact, reach deep into the Underworld. A rumble begins beneath the earth and rises to a mighty roar. The maidens scatter, but Persephone still clutches the plant. The earth opens and out rushes the chariot of the Underworld king, Pluto. He catches Persephone in his arms and disappears with her, to the Shadowlands.

Wringing her hands and calling, Demeter scours the land for her daughter. Meanwhile everything begins to die, for the caring hand of Demeter is withdrawn from the earth. Hearing where her daughter has been taken, she besieges Olympus, demanding that she be released. Such is the importance of the goddess that her request is taken seriously. Negotiations among the Olympian deities result in Persephone's return to the upper air for eight months of the year. When she departs for the Underworld during the other four months, her mother Demeter, the nature goddess, mourns her, and so the land is plunged into winter.

It is most unacceptable from a feminist perspective – or, indeed, from any viewpoint that values freedom – to have rape enshrined as an action that brings about the seasonal cycle. However, if we seek a more subtle interpretation, Persephone's fate appears very different. What is it really that takes Persephone so much by storm? And Pluto, chthonic Underworld deity that he is, is he not sent by the great Earth Mother – another aspect of the Goddess – in whose depths he dwells? The various characters in myths can often be regarded as different aspects of the same dynamic and as different forces within a person's individuality. Astrologically, the planet Pluto rules the sign of Scorpio – a Water sign of profound sensuality and passion, generally regarded as 'feminine' and expressing yin energies, along with all the other Water and Earth signs.

The abduction of the maiden Persephone – also called Kore – can be seen as a metaphor for the onset of the storms of puberty. Now there is a 'death' to the comfortable world of childhood. Entry into the 'underworld' of the personality takes place at this time. We lose our 'innocence', leaving the fairy castles of childhood to enter the dramas of birth, sex and death. These are all connected, in that they transform us, earth us, show us our mortality and yet connect us to something greater. Before the twentieth century each woman approaching labour knew quite well that she risked her life. There is still a brutality about giving birth that is glossed over by patronising midwives and pretty birth-announcement cards. Giving birth is a contact with the dark Goddess, and the fact that this is not honoured in the least may lie behind much of the post-natal 'baby blues'. The initiation experience has not been given due place.

Sex, as a natural prerequisite for pregnancy and birth, also connects us to inexorable shadowy forces within. It's a truism that 'you always hurt the one you love' – no one can hurt you like she or he can, no one else has the hotline to your most vulnerable nooks and crannies. Hate and love are very close together. Orgasm has been described as 'the little death'. We lose ourselves in those we love, and if the relationship is basically a good one, we find ourselves in new form. Sex is an initiation.

Death is the final initiation – no one can be sure in their 'rational' consciousness what lies beyond, but we have a sense that birth, sex and death are connected in meaning beyond the obvious. Patriarchal approach, fearing this dark domain, has reduced birth to a medical event, made regulations to control sex and produced a clearly defined description of life after death, as though it merely involved removal to some heavenly hotel or infernal basement. Of course, this is simplistic, but nonetheless it forms the basis of much belief – or non-belief. The myth of Persephone reassures us that death is followed by rebirth.

The gods decree that Persephone may return to the upper world if she has eaten nothing in Hades, but she has eaten of a pomegranate. This means she must return periodically below ground, as the seed does, for the pomegranate that seals her fate is a symbol of fertility.

The story of Persephone is perhaps better seen as an encounter with the Goddess within and without. Persephone discovers other laws, laws that are about the forces of Nature, the forces of passion, destruction, transformation, laws that manmade rules can never tame, or even make sense of. The fact that Persephone and Demeter are goddesses themselves reminds us that the Goddess exists *within* the drama, immanent in this as in all else. She does not decree it and stand aside.

There are times in life when all we can do is surrender to these forces and let them change us. Demeter the sorrowing mother, Persephone the frightened (yet excited?) girl-woman, Pluto the implacable rapist – all these are aspects of the same internal drama, and we may find each within ourselves and within our lives at crucial points. When we feel compelled to a course of action, sorrowing at what this choice may lose us, frightened, yet excited, then we are in the process of an inner change that is as valid as the transition from summer to winter. As Persephone becomes Queen of the Underworld, so we come into greater power as a result of such experiences. We can be sure that the Goddess is teaching us something.

Inanna and Ereshkigal

Inanna (also called Ishtar) was the Sumerian great goddess of heaven and earth. A mighty queen, she lusted, fought and dispensed the laws of civilisation, called the 'me'. These are not so much moral precepts as the natural, archetypal order of existence, yet Inanna is seen as bestowing justice and giving comfort.

Powerful and wilful, the heavenly queen decides that she will journey to the Underworld to visit her sister Ereshkigal, who rules there. Like all who seek to enter the deathly realms, she is challenged at the gate. Hearing of her presumption, her pregnant sister Ereshkigal who has recently been widowed, falls into a rage. She insists that Inanna receives the same treatment as all visitors. So one piece of Inanna's splendid attire is removed at each of the seven gates, and she is brought before her sister 'naked and bowed low'. Not placated, Ereshkigal kills her and hangs her body on a meathook where it turns into a rotting carcass.

Three days later, as she has failed to return, her assistant Ninshubar rouses gods and humans for her rescue. Finally Enki, god of the waters and wisdom, fashions two hermaphrodite mourners from the red earth beneath his fingernails. These little beings slip unnoticed into the Netherworld. Coming upon Ereshkigal, groaning with her birth-pangs and with despair and grief, the little mourners empathise with Ereshkigal's sorrow, bearing it with her and validating the feelings of the lonely goddess. Not seeking to soothe with false comfort, giving the emotions due recognition, they are the first therapists! Ereshkigal, healed and grateful, feels moved to restore Inanna to life.

Through each of the seven gates surges the great goddess, reclaiming her brilliant regalia, item by item. Too bright for the eye to behold, she returns to the Upperworld savage with anger, surrounded by demons who are searching to take back a substitute for her, to the Netherworld. Finding her consort Dumuzi (also called Tammuz) has not mourned her, but has been feasting and generally enjoying himself, she sets upon him the baleful eye of death. Dumuzi is slain, and takes her place, but his sister, Geshtinanna, pleads for him, and so Inanna decrees that they shall divide the time and each spend half the year in the Underworld. Yet Inanna mourns Dumuzi when he is lost to her – and so Dumuzi/Tammuz is an aspect of the dying and resurrecting vegetation god, the Son-Lover that has become familiar to us.

Commentary

Inana's descent seems, on the face of it, to be more a voluntary choice than that of Persephone, but there are many similarities. This is an older tale, raw and grim, with death and decomposition explicit precursors to the rebirth into a new consciousness.

Ereshkigal has much to teach 'daughters of the patriarchy' – those of us who have taken on the role of bright, intellectual achiever, or who have embraced the socially approved role of 'nice' mother and wife. In living these roles we amputate the archaic Feminine, the abode of Ereshkigal, that is our true source of power. She is the matriarchal consciousness that sees death and life as transformations that are part of a continuum, growing seed, reaping, dying, growing again, whereas to the patriarchy death is the destruction of life, to be controlled by 'moral' order and kept at a distance. Of Ereshkigal's domain Sylvia Perera (see Further Reading) has this to say:

In those depths we are given a sense of the one cosmic power; there we are moved and taught through the intensity of our effects that there is a living balance process. On those levels the conscious ego is overwhelmed by passion and numinous images. And, though shaken, even destroyed as we knew ourselves, we are recoalesced in a new pattern and spewed back into ordinary life. That journey is the goal of the initiation mysteries and of work on the astral plane in magic, even as it is the goal of therapeutic regression (for both men and women) . . . the story of Innanna's descent is the revelation of an initiation ritual, and it is directly relevant to feminine experience today.

When we enter this 'underworld' we do so stripped of our achievements and adorments, we are quite naked before this primitive power. While there we must submit to a 'death' of part of ourselves, enter a 'dark night of the soul' where we can control nothing, and must simply wait as if for the process of digestion – all such autonomic functions are Ereshkigal's territory. The only help we may receive, or perhaps give ourselves, is that of acceptance and perhaps validation, as Enki's mourners do. At length we are released into a new power. We may feel free to show fury, take action, where formerly we were unconscious. Inanna retakes power from Dumuzi, where perhaps she had formerly given too much away to a man who appreciated her only as a giver of pleasure and fertility. Dumuzi's actions can also be seen as the challenge of an equal, the lover who tests our sense of Self and activates our complexes, and as such he is reinstated, but only at due time and as part of natural law, i.e. that of the seasons.

An example

For those of us who have endured harrowing experiences, much of the myth may make immediate sense. However, in case it seems obscure and theoretical, let us invent a real-life example:

A woman, in love with a man, walks in the rosy glow of love, the achievement of romantic conquest. She may also feel rewarded by motherhood. However, too much of her is 'asleep' and being lived out for her by her partner, and too much may be repressed in filling a patriarchally determined role. She is being a 'good girl' and has lost contact with her more primitive side.

Gradually she becomes aware that the relationship is not fulfiling her, or (more frequently) the man behaves hurtfully and rejects her – he is not as she supposed him to be and he cannot play the role that she needs. Now may begin the 'underworld descent'. Stripped bit by bit of all that formerly gave life meaning, she stands naked and defenceless before her inner realisations, yet she cannot escape. Like the corpse on the meathook she is stuck – how many of us are 'stuck' by our obsessions and fixations in a hell of our own making, knowing our mistake, yet unable to escape? And so we suffer horribly. It feels like part of us dies, perhaps the decision-making part, and like Ereshkigal we can only feel miserable, waiting for something, we know not what, to take its course. Hopefully, in due time, with the correct, non-invasive help, something shifts. Bit by bit our woman in the example realises that the way she has been living has meant a repression of much of her potential. Her harrowing experience can be seen as the only way to find release, which she may have unconsciously been seeking – and now she is stronger. Like Inanna she is 'surrounded by demons' – she has reclaimed her self-worth and with it her wrath. Seeing the lover in a new light and now able to function alone on the basis of her own instincts, she breaks off the relationship, or restructures it in a more suitable form, from a position of greater power.

This example is not original, nor is it complete, but it is one which many of us may recognise in our friends or ourselves – although sadly many people remain in an 'underworld' of depression for many years. Although love affairs are generally a prime cause for this sort of experience it can come in all sorts of guises, triggered by career moves, non-erotic relationships, bereavement, or simply coming upon us in a depression we cannot understand.

And so the descent of the Goddess teaches us about our own depths – the 'underworld' of our complexes and desires – things we may shrink from but which have much to offer us if braved

– and we do not always have a choice about 'braving' them! As women we have access to pre-verbal, intensely creative yet scary domains that exist before judgement and logic enter the scene. Ultimately, this is about restoring our own 'natural order' which has to do with our power as women – self-validating, raw femaleness. On a collective level, we may understand that the dark Goddess realms, where natural law flows and throbs through subterranean passages, where the inexorable rules of life and death are enthroned, cannot be avoided but need to be incorporated into any worldview that attempts to be complete. These are the pre-verbal realms of instinct, the cycles of decay and growth. If they are not given due honour as the foundations of our lives there is the risk that they will open up and swallow us – as the earth closed over the chariot of Pluto, as a holocaust of war or pollution could claim us, if we remain unconscious of the importance of these areas.

Practice

At the end of this chapter we may ask ourselves how much room we give in our lives to the dark Goddess within, to Ereshkigal, to that part of us which is not 'nice' but which really knows about life. Do we honour our gut feelings? How far have we confined ourselves within roles that are socially acceptable, when they may not be an expression of our true selves? What bits of us do we relegate to an inner 'underworld', too afraid even to look at them ourselves? Exploring these parts of ourselves is a long journey. You may find it helpful and interesting to think about the contents of this chapter in relation to your life. If it does not seem totally relevant, take from it only the parts that seem interesting and thought provoking for you.

7

goddess of many faces

I am the stream and the cup that is filled,
I am the bleeding and I am the blood,
I am the woman who cries on the rock,
I am the child who grows wise in the sun,
I am the moon as she rises to full
I am the sister who comes from the south
I am the dance of the babe in the womb
I am the Spirit who breathes on the land . . .

'I (Am the Spirit)', Carolyn Hillyer, from the album *Heron Valley*, Seventh Wave Music, 1993

The Goddess permeates the whole of life, and comes to us in many guises. Let us look at some of Her manifestations.

Mistress of magic and healing

Goddess worship leads us naturally into magical realms for several reasons. Firstly, it is about instinctual levels where the rules of logic do not function. This does not mean that we indulge in silly superstition, but it does mean we perceive hidden meanings and connections – forces that are not necessarily 'scientific'. This is only a short step from valuing intuition – traditionally a feminine sphere. Secondly, worship of the Goddess means actively encouraging personal revelation and mysticism. From this perspective it becomes evident that all is connected on the cosmic web, and so any action affects the whole – magic is the art of manipulating these connections. Thirdly, those who worship the Goddess feel encouraged to develop their own potential in whatever way seems right. The Goddess does not ask us to bow our heads, humble ourselves as supplicants. She encourages us to strengthen our own wills and to create the life circumstances that we want and need. Magic is 'the art of causing change to occur in conformity with the will'.

There were many motives for the medieval witch hunts, greed and paranoia being two of these. Principally, masculine, logos-orientated approaches fear and denigrate the primal, intuitional and ecstatic qualities of the older Goddess worship. Witchcraft is, in essence, Goddess worship. It has nothing whatever to do with the devil, in whom witches do not believe. Nor is it evil, by any definition other than that of those who call anything that does not subscribe to their dogmas 'evil'. 'Witch' is a highly charged word even today, and many people are very wary about its use. However, it is a word that throbs with raw, feminine power. Many herbalists, midwives, healers and early feminists (as well as an overwhelming number of ordinary people who were merely unfortunate) died in the name of the word 'witch'. Witches are almost always healers of some description. Today witches are growing in numbers – or is it that they are now able to become more public? The subject is explored fully in *Witchcraft – a Mobius Guide* in this series. For our witchcraft myths, let us look at two Greek goddesses, Hecate and Circe.

Hecate

Hecate is an evocative figure, mysterious and sinister. Originally she was a triple goddess, but she has come down to us principally as Crone. She was goddess of crossroads, because there one can look three ways, and it was at crossroads that offerings were left for her. As she stalked the darkness her worshippers would retreat indoors to hold feasts in her honour and whisper the ways of sorcery. Hecate is not a deity to be taken lightly!

She was originally a pre-Olympian Titan, but she retained her power into classical Greece and could grant or withhold anything she wished. She commanded the ghostly hordes of the dead and she presided over the secrets of regeneration. Her animals were the dog and the serpent, and the inky time of dark Moon was her domain, when she would sit, humming at the crossroads, stirring her cauldron. A later story tells that she was daughter of Zeus and Hera, the Olympian monarchs. She stole her mother's rouge to give to Europa – one of her father's many mistresses. Fleeing from her mother's anger she came to Earth and hid in the house of a woman in childbirth, from where the Cabeiri, Underworld smith divinities, transported her to the Acheron and plunged her into the flood. Thus she became a great Underworld goddess.

This is a tale of mischief and breached boundaries that seems trivial. Probably it has been given a patriarchal slant. We can detect within it links between the transformative powers of birth, sexuality and death. Hecate is not a moral figure, nor does she possess much filial loyalty. Rather she is part of the shaping hand of Fate. She understands that her father's love affairs are part of destiny, she is linked with the demi-gods of the transformative art of smithcraft, and she 'hides' where a baby is born. Hecate's message is that darkness precedes light, death is part of life and that true, transformative knowledge comes from encompassing both. When we are at a loss to understand our world, needing to access deep parts of ourselves to get by, then we may look out on a moonless night and call to Hecate, to guide us into our depths and out of them again.

Circe

Daughter of the brilliant Sun and of the Cretan Queen Pasiphae, mother of the Minotaur, Circe lived on the island of Aeaea, in a stone house encircled by lions and wolves. The wandering hero Odysseus/Ulysses succumbed to her charms and fathered her two sons. His men were turned into swine by her spells. Thus Circe shows us our animal natures and how perspectives can be altered, so that what was familiar becomes strange and vice versa, and all we thought we could do recedes, leaving us with qualities we may have neglected. The pig is a fertile creature, often associated with the Underworld. Mistress of secret twists and turns, we may call on Circe when we know the direct approach will not do and we need a little magic to get by.

Transcendence

Transcendence (i.e. the rising above and seeing beyond the everyday outlook into the realms of the eternal) is not merely the province of Fathergod, although with goddesses it takes on rather a different perspective. Goddesses are rarely depicted as repudiating the physical body, and Goddess worship encourages transcendence through the sacredness of the physical and not by regarding it as inferior. Athene, Greek goddess of wisdom, pictured as being born from the head of her father, Zeus, in what can be regarded as an outrageous travesty of birth, still has her earthy and Underworld connections in the shape of the snake-headed Gorgon that she wears on her breastplate.

Birds, one of the earliest Goddess symbols, are signs of transcendence. Let us look at the tale of a Welsh goddess to illustrate this.

Blodeuedd

Blodeuedd was the beautiful flower-faced goddess made from meadowsweet, oak and broom by the magicians Math and Gwydion, to be wife to Lleu Llaw Gyffes who had the doom laid on him by his mother the goddess Arianrhod that he would never marry. This fate had been decreed because of the magicians' earlier mischief, but, undaunted, they found a way around it. Neither they nor the fond husband, however, thought to ask this enchanting goddess if she wished to marry Lleu!

Although ethereally beautiful, the ruthless law of Nature informed Blodeuedd, who was, after all, made from plant-life. She fell passionately in love with Gronw Pebr, a huntsman she spotted from her castle window, and they plotted to kill Lleu, who could only be slain in unusual circumstances due to his divine nature.

After the death of Lleu, Blodeuedd is turned into an owl, a creature that haunts the night, far from soft beds of lovers, rending its prey with its cruel beak. Lleu is turned into a wounded eagle, the rotting flesh dropping from his sores being eaten by a sow. Gwydion restores him to be avenged on Gronw, but by night in his stony castle he hears the lone voice of the owl and longs for the sweet arms of his flower maid.

Being turned into a bird of prey may sound like a punishment, and so may have been the intention. However, let us remember that the Goddess, as bird, was shown as laying the World Egg. The owl is a resolution of opposites, the flower maid and the traitoress, the rending beak of destruction balancing the generative powers of the womb, and this union means transcendence and wisdom. Also associated with Athene, the owl has long meant wisdom, beautiful night bird, straight from the mysteries of the dark Goddess. As for Lleu's eagle, an eagle too is a symbol of transcendence, but of a more polarised sort. Wounded, its flesh eaten by a sow, we are reminded that all who wish to rise must remember death and decomposition is part of the cycle. Blodeuedd reminds us that true wisdom respects natural law, while searching for the broad vistas of Spirit.

Divine protectress – Kuan-Yin

We may call on the Goddess to help us in our hour of need, for in so doing we conjure Her presence into our souls. Many goddesses are protective, and the Catholic figure of the Virgin Mary has long been depicted as interceding for the souls of humans. Chinese Buddhism offers the figure of the bodhisattva, Kuan-Yin, as a picture of redeeming, caring femininity. Kuan-Yin is the most powerful deity in the Chinese pantheon, and her name means 'she who hears the weeping world'.

A bodhisattva is one who has attained complete enlightenment, but rather than progress into a state of pure energy and union with the divine source, such a one returns to Earth to help all those in need. Kuan-Yin has promised to remain with us until every living creature has found enlightenment. Her name alone is an invocation of peace, mercy and protection from all harm. When we are afraid, confused, threatened in any way spiritually or physically, then we may call on Kuan-Yin to surround us with her light and bathe us in the flow of her love.

The love Goddess – Aphrodite

The Goddess blesses all acts of love and pleasure. Certainly She smiles on sexual love, for this offers pinnacles of human pleasure and also forms an entrance to Her mysteries. For an example of a goddess of love we are inevitably drawn to Greek Aphrodite.

Although Aphrodite was trivialised in the emerging Olympian pantheon, her power was awesome, and even the King of the Gods, Zeus, was at her mercy when she so decreed. Aphrodite was called 'foam-born' because she was born of the sea, when the genitals of her father Uranus, castrated by his son, Chronos, fell into the waves. Her birth is the subject of Botticelli's well-known masterpiece *The Birth of Venus*. Aphrodite is really a descendant of Sumerian Inanna, Assyro-Babylonian Ishtar, Phoenician Astarte and Hebrew Ashera – she evolves from a long line of imposing goddesses of the Middle East.

Aphrodite is the patroness of pure lust and physical delight – she is no 'dumb blonde' but epitomises the power of sex that energises every corner of the cosmos. Legend tells of her love for the beautiful youth Adonis ('Adonai' means 'Lord' in Hebrew) who was an avid huntsman. She begged him to give up this dangerous sport, but he laughed and blithely continued. Adonis is gored to death by a wild bear and descends to Hades, where Queen Persephone, enchanted by his beauty, refuses to relinquish him to the pleading goddess. At length agreement is made that Adonis must live four months alone, four months with Aphrodite and four months with Persephone. The familiar theme of the dying and resurrecting God, consort to the Goddess, is here again. Patricia Monaghan (see Further Reading) sees in Aphrodite, as in other great goddesses, the '. . . symbolic description of the hopeless love of the earth herself for the life she continually produces and inevitably consumes'. We can see Aphrodite as the goddess whose passionate love restores even the dead to life.

White Buffalo Woman

Native Americans tell of how White Buffalo Woman brought the secret of the peace pipe to humans. The buffalo is an animal given much honour, for it supplied all the needs of the native Americans, giving flesh to be eaten, skin for clothing and tents, and bones for many uses. Thus this goddess came as a representation of the powers of Life.

Clad in white and decked with rich embroidery, she first appeared to two young men. Despite the warnings of his friend one of the pair rushed to embrace her. Smiling, she received him and a white cloud arose from nowhere to cover their embrace. When it receded the woman stood alone with the skeleton of the man at her feet.

In awe the other youth led her to the village, and as they walked she told him that his companion had received just what he sought. When she arrived at the village she conveyed the ceremonies of the sacred pipe to the people. The pipe represents the union of male and female, in the stem and bowl, and the smoke that passes through is the informing, connecting Spirit. Telling the people always to remember to honour the Earth Mother, she changed into a white buffalo and disappeared.

This story illustrates the power of sexuality as a unifying principle. It also shows its destructive potential when misused, and its subtle link with the death process – as the first youth found out!

Goddesses of destruction

The Goddess incorporates death as well as life, destruction as well as creation. This can be a sticking point in our culture, committed as we consciously are to the preservation of life at any price, and it is all too easy to condemn as 'evil' anything that destroys. However, metabolism involves katabolism as well as anabolism, decay and compost fertilise new growth and it is death that gives life its meaning. It must also be said that despite our supposed reverence for life, nurture and positivity, ours is the most violent society in recorded history, with the capability of global destruction. Clearly something is not quite right.

One of the problems, of course, with embracing the light, so to speak, is that something then falls into shadow. Identify solely with the light side of the dark/light polarity, the other side is then sought outside us, instead of finding honesty and balance within. Unfortunate, unpleasant events are seen as the fault of someone or something else and so we find ourselves in a fight to the death, embodying the very murderous power we sought to extinguish. Of course, there is no easy answer to this, but we may begin by giving due honour to the Divine Destructress, for she is Goddess indeed, and though we do not seek to behave like Her, any more than we can imitate any other goddess, yet She can show us how to make peace with the darker aspects of ourselves and when to make endings in our lives.

Kali

One of most terrifying of all goddesses is the Hindu Kali, and legend says that it is her dance that will end the world. She dances with Shiva, Lord of the Dance, and she dances best and most thrillingly on the cold, dead flesh of her victims. Kali wears dismembered bodies as jewellery. She has three eyes, her tongue juts from her coal-black face and she carries death in her womb. Kali was created as a result of a threat by a demon to the goddess Parvati – golden goddess of sexual love. As fury mounted in Parvati, from her body sprang Kali who quickly killed the demon – but now thrust into the world Kali could not be destroyed or controlled. She was sometimes honoured by bloody sacrifice.

To Hindus all goddesses are ultimately one goddess, aspects of the great goddess Devi. However, Kali is one of her most favoured representations. This may seem strange indeed unless we understand Kali's spiritual significance. Patricia Monaghan writes: 'As a symbol of the worst we can imagine . . . she offers us a chance to face down our own terror of annihilation . . . Kali . . . is a blissful goddess. Once faced and understood Kali frees her worshippers of all fear and becomes . . . the most comforting of goddesses.'

The Valkyries

The supernatural battle maidens, flying over the carnage of war and evoked so stirringly by Wagner, have an older and even more powerful essence. These were the goddesses who wove the web of war with spears, arrows, human heads and blood, determining the result of the battle that was to come. Their grisly work completed, they flew forth like vultures to devour the bodies of the dead. A law unto themselves, they taught magic to the heroes they decided to save, and they have much in common with the Greek Fates. Sometimes they took on the shapes of ravens or wolves, but only those with second sight could see them, for ordinary mortals could see only the flickering Northern Lights licking the skies over the battlefield.

The Warrior Goddess

The Goddess can also appear as a martial adept. This is rather different from the all-encompassing destructive powers of Kali, which exemplify very primal forces. Rather the Warrior Goddess is about assertion – the indomitable will that fights for right and identity. This has often been regarded as a masculine characteristic. However, Sylvia Perera (see Further Reading) likens Ereshkigal, whom we met in Chapter 6, to the 'female yang'. Ereshkigal's peg can be seen as a 'female phallus' that may fill the empty womb with a 'new and holy attitude to life'. This is a force more earthed and grounded than the male, and yet if necessary it can imbue a woman with fighting spirit. The Amazons are perhaps the best known as female warriors, but there are other examples.

Scathach

Scathach was the 'shadowy one', a goddess who inhabited an island off the Scottish coast and to whom all the great heroes, including Cuchulain, came to be instructed in the arts of war. She was mistress of magical skills that could make a warrior invincible, and she was famous for her 'salmon leap' which could gain access to impregnable heights. Scathach suggests that women possess many secrets about self-assertion and combat.

Fertility

It seems almost superfluous to identify fertility as an aspect of the Goddess, for it is so basic to all forms of Her. However, some goddesses exemplify this characteristic more than others. Scandinavian Freya is one example.

Freya

The goddesses Freya and Frigg are often confused, and although Freya seems to embody sexual passion, while Frigg is about motherhood, it is possible that they are one and the same person. Freya led the Vanir, matriarchal and agricultural deities, and she was modelled on an earlier goddess, Nerthus, whose effigy was carried through towns in a wagon drawn by cows. Freya imparted the magical secrets of Seidr – shamanistic and herbalistic lore – to Odin. Odin was also said to be her husband in his aspect as Odr. The volva, priestesses of the Vanir, seem to have survived the incoming patriarchal deities into the ninth century CE, and their practice is revived in the Northern Tradition of contemporary paganism. As goddess of love and death, Freya seems to be of very ancient origin, and in her aspect as Frigg she is the mother of the dying god Baldur, who seems akin to many other vegetation deities, Sons of the Mother.

Cybele

The worship of Cybele survived into the Christian era in Rome. Cybele is one of the best-known Near Eastern goddesses – a great earth mother, clad in all the colours of the earth, full-breasted and carrying corn and keys. She loved her grandson Attis, who was unfaithful to her, but no secrets could be kept from Cybele, who was truly the all-knowing earth herself. Attis went mad and in an agony of remorse, castrated himself and bled to death from his wound. Yet again, Attis is a vegetation deity, and although myth does not specifically mention his rebirth, it is implied in the festival of joy that marked the new growing season, celebrated in Rome. Initiates worked themselves into a frenzy, amputating their own genitals in honour of the goddess – a practice sternly discouraged by the masculine Romans! As goddess of holy madness Cybele embodies the black heart of Nature and abides only by the primal laws that, to ordinary consciousness, are lawlessness itself.

Lady of the Beasts

In all her myriad forms the Goddess has been shown in association with various animals. These animals are a 'showing forth' of the power of the Goddess, a manifestation of Her design. In addition, animals are vibrant, living symbols – totems that can give us access to our instinctual and intuitional skills.

The **bird** shows the Goddess as Creatrix (laying the world-egg) linking earth, sky and the waters in the mysteries of flight.

The **serpent** suggests, by its spiralling shape, passage into and out of the visible world. Snakes shed their skin, so suggesting rebirth and female sexual rhythms. Birds and snakes appeared in association with the Goddess from the Stone Age.

The **lion** shows the sheer power of the Great Mother, imperious, a fierce protector and mother. The Egyptian goddesses Sekhmet and Bast (who has the head of a cat, and represents gentler manifestations) are brought to mind.

The **dog**, intelligent, energetic, with an almost magical sense of smell, was honoured in relation to the Goddess from the Neolithic era. Dogs wail at the Moon and the Goddess Hecate is linked with them.

The **butterfly** is a symbol of transformation and rebirth. The shape of the butterfly is reminiscent of the double-headed Creatan axe, the labrys. Cutting two ways, the labrys suggests both death and renewal, and also resembles the labia of the female genital area.

The **spider** – many goddesses are shown as spinning and weaving the threads of life and destiny: Arachne, Athene, Arianrhod and Ariadne being but a few. The web of the spider is a metaphor for the Cosmic Web.

The **fish**, coming from the waters, signifies feminine wisdom. Many goddesses came from the sea, for example Aphrodite and the Syrian Atargatis.

The **pig** is often linked with the Underworld. The pig's association with agriculture may be due to its habit of rooting in the soil with its snout. A fertile animal that sometimes consumes its farrow, the pig is associated with the goddess Cerridwen who exemplifies death and rebirth. Cerridwen is pictured stirring a cauldron with a magic brew of wisdom, intended for her ugly son, Afagddu. She leaves this in the care of little Gwion, but some drops spill on to his finger, so he receives the gift of inspiration. Cerridwen chases Gwion and they both change form many times until she eats him as a grain of wheat, while she is in the form of a hen. Nine months later she gives birth to the legendary bard Taliesin. So Cerridwen is a fearsome but potent muse. She is especially recalled at Samhain, and her sow symbol used to represent her.

The **horse** may exemplify raw earth-power. White horses are etched on many English hillsides, and the goddess Rhiannon, White Mare of the Sea, is pictured riding a white horse. It is said she leads the people of the Hollow Hills on moonlit nights, snaring careless mortals with enchantment.

The **bull** often represents the Son-Lover of the Goddess, and the bull's head looks like a cross-section of womb and ovaries. Cows and bulls are associated with fertility. Indian myth tells of the birth of the universe through the churning of the milk of the Goddess, the celestial cow Surabhi. In India cows are sacred to this day.

The above are merely samples of Goddess-animals and their significance. We may see importance in all animals as Her gifts.

Practice

Perhaps the most longed-for aspect of the Goddess is that of the love goddess, Aphrodite. If we need to attract love into our lives we may like to dedicate a small shelf or table-top in our house to the goddess, decorating it with shells and flowers. On a night when the Moon is waxing, light a rose-coloured candle on your altar and imagine that love is entering your life. Try not to be too specific about the type of person, certainly restrain yourself from directing your energies at any specific individual, however desirable they may seem. If you wish for friendship call on the goddess as Aphrodite-Urania, or her Roman counterpart,

Venus. If you can do this at sundown, when the planet Venus is on the horizon, so much the better. Repeat this until your wishes are answered.

An Aphrodite visualisation

The ancient temples of Aphrodite were located in wild places that naturally inspired awe – a comment on the nature of this goddess. If you have a question about love you may like to approach the goddess in this visualisation exercise – so much the better if you can first record it on a tape. Firstly, make yourself relaxed, in an position that is comfortable for you, and ensure that you won't be disturbed. Formulate your question clearly before you start: You are on a beach, covered with shells, pebbles and sand. The blue ocean swells and the waves pound in slow rhythm. Look around and take note of all you see.

Short pause

You notice a path winds up and up, towards the heights of cliffs that rise above the beach. You decide that you will take this path. Up and up you climb. Parts of the cliff path seem treacherous. Sheer drops suddenly appear, down to the beach below. The scree slips beneath your feet. Branches catch at you and thorns scratch. The way is rough and hard and all the time you hear the sounds of the pounding ocean, far below. Keep following this path and take note of all you see.

Short pause

Now the ground levels out and you find that you are walking on soft grass. The distant waves sound like gentle drum beats and there is a tinkling sound, as if wind chimes are trembling in the breeze. Beautiful flowers grow at the edges of the path and the air is sweet with their fragrance. Soon you come into a clearing. There is a green grotto opposite you, surrounded by roses. Pearly sea-shells are arranged around it. Take some time to get to know this place.

Short pause

Ask that the goddess Aphrodite may come to you. You may sense her, see her, hear her, or feel her presence. Ask her the question that you have come with and wait patiently for the answer in whatever form it comes – you may hear or see something, or be shown a symbol. Do not try to make any interpretation at this moment.

Short pause

When it seems right, thank the goddess and make your farewell. Come down the path back to the beach – your descent will be smoother than the upward journey. Remain a while on the sea shore, and then come back to everyday awareness when you are ready.

Write down what you have experienced. If you don't understand the full importance at present it may come to you later. If you did not receive an answer or if the goddess did not come to you, try again another day. Take a note of all you did see, hear or sense, for there may be significances there that you have missed.

8

the goddess
lives on

To the high land they have journeyed
Words of truth and eyes of vision
A hundred thousand women
And a hundred thousand heartbeats . . .
Will you dance with me sweet daughters
Within the many circles of our lives
Held together by two drumbeats
Heart drum of the mother
Heart drum of the child

Carolyn Hillyer, 'Two Drumbeats', from the album *Heron Valley*, Seventh Wave Music, 1993

As the Bronze Age gave way to the Iron Age the 'warrior consciousness' grew – that masculine, achievement and conquest-orientated approach that has been with us ever since. Many of us are unhappy with much that we see, from Cruise missiles to 'sales targets' yet we are not totally aware how old fashioned it is, and how our immature philosophies lag behind our technological prowess, creating the potential for a massive disaster. In growing numbers people are seeking a new 'Goddess consciousness' that detaches from external conquest and emphasises the inner light of the Spirit and the interconnectedness of all. Ransom and Bernstein (see Further Reading) write: 'In a masculine-based reality, you struggle with the fates; you don't acknowledge that all cause and all reality is based on your own self-perception or responses to the universe . . . When . . . you accept that the power of birth, death, and regeneration of the Self is in your consciousness, you are definitely on the path of the Goddess.'

Our goal-emphasis has not been 'wrong' for it has brought us much in the way of comfort and progress. Also it has been part of a process of sharpening the consciousness of each individual as to her or his uniqueness. It would not be appropriate to attempt to return to the state of primitive participation in Nature that may have been general in the Palaeolithic era. We need to develop something new that answers our needs today. Meanwhile, along our journey through ego-centred action-orientated centuries, the Goddess has been with us. Concealed, disguised, often demonised, misunderstood and feared, She has been there, keeping hope alight in the hearts that receive Her.

The Goddess in the Old Testament

The nefarious nature of woman is exemplified by Eve, who tempts Adam with the apple, against the express command of God. This results in the expulsion from the Garden of Eden, and women have laboured under this crime for many centuries. By implication, however, the power of woman is immense, for

Adam seemingly has no mind of his own! This outlook still prevails in attitudes regarding rape, that die hard. The myth that men are not responsible for their actions when confronted by a seductive woman halts with blaming the woman and does not extend to questions about male self-determination! Sex has often been held to be the concealed theme in the expulsion from Eden – an evil into which woman tempted man. However, there are other interpretations.

The serpent speaks to Eve, and the serpent is a very ancient and powerful symbol of wisdom. Could it be that woman led man to greater consciousness? Women, as carriers of the life-force, tillers, sowers, reapers, weavers, potters, ushered the human race out of the hunter-gatherer aeons into a developing society. Could it have been the feminine, reflective quality that differentiated consciousness, thus rupturing the bliss of primal 'oneness' that existed before? As the human race developed the ability to think and feel a sense of Self, so the agony of separation and aloneness came upon us – a feeling of being split off from the Divine, the totality. That is and always has been frightening, and perhaps woman was the primary scapegoat. This may be partly because she is closer to what has been lost. Or the blaming of woman may rest in the fact that she, by her closer identification with instinct, represents an ever-present threat to the primacy of the ego. Leading the way out of mystical participation and/or representing it, as a threat of the overwhelming non-rational or a reminder of lost bliss, woman became 'bad news'.

The Hebrew language has no word for Goddess, but the references in the Old Testament to the anger of Yahweh at strange gods are hard to understand if there were no effigies and sacred places of the Goddess in existence. When the Hebrew tribes settled in Canaan many took on older beliefs. Cashford and Baring (see Further Reading) tell us: 'Despite the efforts of the prophets to eradicate the old beliefs, the image of the Goddess survived. In Canaan, as in the surrounding countries, the mythology of the Goddess and her son-lover was the most deeply rooted aspect of religious belief . . .'

Some of the canaanite goddesses were the Mother Goddess Asherah, Anath, goddess of the hunt and Astarte, Queen of Heaven, who is similar to Inanna and Ishtar. The Old Testament does not give a true impression of how prevailing was the worship of these goddesses. Goddesses also appear disguised as cherubim and the people of Israel are, interestingly, referred to as the 'bride of Yahweh', as if this warlike Fathergod just had to have a consort somewhere! The Feminine also appears as Sophia, Wisdom, as in Proverbs 3:13–18: 'Happy is the man that findeth wisdom . . . She is more precious than rubies . . . She is a tree of life to them that lay hold upon her . . .' Most strikingly, the beautiful eroticism of the Song of Solomon echoes the Sacred Marriage theme of Goddess and God, monarch and land (or the High Priestess that stood for the land):

Behold thou art fair my love; behold thou art fair; thou hast dove's eyes. Behold thou art fair, my beloved, yea, pleasant: also our bed is green

(1:15,16)

The fig tree putteth forth her green figs and the vines with the tender grape give good smell. Arise my love, my fair one, and come away

(2:13)

So images of the Divine Feminine persisted, yet they were not specially enshrined. Deity stood outside creation and pronounced dogmas that were engraved on stone. The old Goddess went underground.

The New Testament and beyond

We have already mentioned how Mary, the mother of Christ, is a form of the Goddess in all but name. Cashford and Baring (see Further Reading) tell us: 'Mary is the unrecognised Mother Goddess of the Christian tradition'. The sacrificial death of Jesus echoes much older themes of sacrificial gods, sons of the Mother Goddess. Great Mothers are associated with the primeval ocean and Mary's name comes from the Latin for sea, *mare*. Effigies of the Black Virgin continue the association of the Goddess with darkness, earth and night – many miracles of healing are linked with this image. The Black Virgin is also associated with Mary Magdalene, the whore, and it is this Mary who first sees the risen Christ, mistaking him for the gardener – the 'gardener' was the name given to the Son-Lover in Sumeria. Suggestions have been made that Mary Magdalene and Christ were lovers – if so, it would be supremely fitting that she should be the first to see Him risen. There is confusion at times between the 'Marys' in the Bible – could it be that they are aspects of the same person/goddess?

Gnostic Christianity blended the mystical elements of the Greek, Egyptian and Hebrew religions in the first centuries CE. This lingered in the Cathar movement and fuelled the study of alchemy and similar subjects in the Middle Ages. Its defining characteristic was the belief in 'gnosis' (i.e. knowledge), which meant direct, inner experience of God. In the Gnostic Gospels the Feminine is exalted as Sophia, the 'first begeteress, Mother of the Universe' – in the Gnostic Church women could teach, prophesy and hold rank, and in the Gospel of Mary she (possibly Mary Magdalene) is shown holding discourse with Peter. The Gnostics emphasised the attainment of inner awakening through insight and personal revelation, rather than belief. They were suppressed by the Emperor Constantine in the fourth century CE – the same Constantine who is called the first Christian Emperor, yet who murdered his son and had his wife boiled alive! Early Christian history seems often at variance with the true message of love and rebirth that was Christ's gift – these may be seen as 'feminine' qualities, which, of course, is not to say that they are not equally available to men.

Up to the present day the image of Mary continues to inspire Catholics. However, Goddess consciousness is reviving in many forms, some specifically about Goddess worship, others concerned more generally with the welfare of the planet. Awareness is growing of the interconnectedness of life in a way that is obviously more specific and conscious than could have been the case in the Stone Age, and from this comes concern for the planet as a whole and for the welfare of indigenous peoples and the deprived all over the globe, not just around the corner. We are questioning our use of environmental resources and cultivating an active respect for the Earth – called 'Green consciousness'. This can be seen as a return of a sense of 'immanence'. However, many people feel that not enough is happening, nor is it happening fast enough. In connection with abuse of the Earth and the Feminine, an old Greek myth comes to mind.

Gaia and Ouranos

Gaia was the ancient Earth Mother of the Greeks, one of the pre-Olympians. Her husband was Ouranos (Uranus) or Sky. Arching over her body, he satisfied her desire for love and children, and so her creativity was released in creatures that were wonderful and monstrous. Ouranos did not like this at all, for he was jealous of his children, and they did not please his eyes. So he insisted that they be shoved back into the womb of Gaia, out of his sight. Naturally this grew most uncomfortable for Gaia, who eventually became very angry. She armed her son, Chronos, with a sickle and plotted with him his father's comeuppance.

As the dark blanket of night drew slowly over the land, Ouranos came to lie with his wife, unaware that his son, one of his despised offspring, was hiding in wait for him in a mountain-top cave. Sore and savage at his father's neglect, Chronos saw his chance and attacked with a cold hatred, sawing off his father's exposed genitals. As the bloodied flesh fell to earth, Gaia gave birth to the Furies, and where the semen mingled with the ocean, lovely Aphrodite was formed. Chronos then took his father's place as king of the Gods, but he did not learn from Ouranos's example. Or perhaps he did, for he set about eating his children, fearing that his own son would supercede him. Zeus escaped, to fulfil this, becoming the later Olympian monarch.

Commentary

There are several interesting metaphors in this story. One is that Ouranos represents the conscious mind that is very often unhappy with the strange contents of the instinctual parts of the psyche. So these are denied, pushed back into darkness and unconsciousness, until, lo and behold, they take possession of us one stormy night when passions we did not know we had erupted, complexes and obsessions claim us or we are strangely bombarded by the feelings of others while we, of course, are 'above that sort of thing'. Detached, inspirational qualities are exemplified by the sign Aquarius, ruled by Uranus. The energies of Uranus are zany and electrifying, but very cerebral, and people who have these charactistics strongly marked may be very creative, yet not like what they create, or finish it properly, or relate to it. What is created never quite matches the celestial inspirations, for it has had to take form in the muddy world of matter, Gaia. As the Age of Aquarius approaches, so perhaps we have to learn to become grounded and to see the wisdom in earthly modifications instead of calling them misshapen. Ironically, this has been more a characteristic of the preceding age, where all formed of matter was inferior. Perhaps now our task is to become truly conscious of the damaging nature of this attitude.

Gaia is the title of the bestselling work by J.E. Lovelock, which puts forward the idea of Earth as a single, living organism of whom humankind may well be the developing nervous system and consciousness of Self. It is intriguing that we are taking up the detached position of Ouranos, as a species, not valuing the Earth, shoving into her all that we have created yet wish to forget, such as nuclear and industrial waste, and choosing to believe that pesticides, pollution, deforestation and all the other travesties do not exist, because most of us can't see them. So preoccupied are we with 'advancement' – and technology is a Uranian function – that we do not see that we are storing up disaster for ourselves that will be revealed inevitably by time. Time, of course, is Chronos – hence 'chronology'. Saturn is the Roman equivalent of Chronos, and the planet Saturn is one of the great time-keepers of the solar system, for the rhythms of Saturn can be detected in people's lives, astrologically. Saturn, with his sickle, is Old Father Time, or the Grim Reaper. Of all the ancient myths, that of Gaia is perhaps the one we most need to heed, before our blind progress is castrated, leaving us as a species, broken, bleeding and perhaps superceded, like Ouranos, like the dinosaurs . . .

Into the future

It is not too simple or too extreme to state that veneration of the Goddess is the only hope for our planet. The loss of a sense of indwelling deity, of the sacredness of the Earth, all of life upon her and of our daily lives has inexorably created the current destructive scenario. This does not mean that everyone must explicitly worship a Goddess, but it does mean that a vivid respect for all things feminine must pervade, for only at soul level can we find healing. Laws are of limited value if there is no feeling behind and if people in their hearts do not have a sense for and care about what is happening.

We have seen an increase in the numbers of women in positions of power, but that hardly satisfies the requirement, for women too are generally logos-centred, subscribing to masculine, hierarchal institutions. Ransom and Bernstein write:

> *Women are taking power in the temporal world, which will change the balance of world power. Hopefully women will present alternative methods of co-operative living. Women in increasing numbers are entering religious, philosophical, and spiritual disciplines. Here lies the hardest struggle. Believe it or not the easiest victories for women are in the business world. The last obstruction will be in the corridors of religious ideas and influence. This is where women will have to fight the hardest due to the dominance of the 'male God archetype' so firmly rooted in the subconscious of the masses.*

It seems that the task is both inner and outer. Inwardly we need to develop 'gnosis' or at least have a respect for personal, spiritual revelation, so that the way is open for it to find us, when the time is right. Outwardly, we need the recognition at a heart level that the planet is a living organism, on whom we, as comparatively humble creatures, depend for our existence. This is recognition that brings quiet joy and wholeness ('holiness') and deep sorrow at what has been wrought. For those of us who are pragmatic and literal, the solid earth may be all the goddess we need. And we need to develop an open-minded respect for the Feminine in all ramifications and manifestations – this means we respect the feminine side of men, too, for all is equally applicable to both sexes.

Much is said and written about the Age of Aquarius. Perhaps the great challenge is to integrate the undeniable benefits of technology and the achieving mind set with the old mystical senses. Too often people take up a stand in support of one or the other, but perhaps we should seek rather to return to that state of sacred living, or participation in all that is, while retaining our ability to function as unique, striving, ego-conscious individuals. That seems to spell something of a move to a new stage of evolution in the human race. To me it sounds like the true union of male and female, Goddess and God – the Sacred Marriage in very truth!

May She, who blesses all, bless you!

Practice

We may seek to bring the Goddess into our lives in many ways. Here are a few suggestions:

Firstly, you can recap on some of the ideas in other chapters, such as lunar observance and studying your menstrual patterns, if you are female. Another important point is to set up a small Goddess shrine in your house as a permanent sacred space. In so doing you are literally 'making room' in your life for the Goddess. If you create a space, something will fill it, something that means love and beauty. Choose a convenient spot for your Goddess shrine and put upon it anything that feels right to you. You may feel tentative at first, but slowly your confidence and consciousness will grow concerning what the Goddess means to you. Goddess statues are becoming more readily available in New Age Shops, and images are available from a resource listed in the back of this book. Choose what appeals to you, whether it may be a complex and expensive image of Isis, or a special stone you found on a walk. A candle is also a good idea. You may take it from there.

Secondly, try to become aware of use of language. It may feel forced to say 'for Godess's sake' instead of 'for

God's sake', but it is worth remembering how our words betray our preconceptions. For instance, in this book I have been careful, where necessary, to say 'her or his' in that order, because the reverse is the norm – and this book hopes to redress the balance a little. As time passes you may be surprised at how your awareness sharpens.

Thirdly, a hackneyed suggestion I know, but it really does help to do our bit for the environment. Don't buy 'rubbish' – stuff that is over-packaged and/or unnecessarily polluting, do recycle, cut car use to a minimum, support environment organisations, write to your Member of Parliament, give what you can (even if only a tiny bit) to charities of your choice, and generally become aware of how your life affects the world around you. There are no rules here, so do not beat yourself about the head with guilty feelings. As you open your heart to the Earth and all that lives, so your priorities will alter, slowly.

Fourthly, if you are aware of the Goddess, show it. Recently a celebrated actress thanked the Goddess, out loud, for an award she received, and was sneered at in the media. The more this happens, the less other people mock and the more they may take notice. Remember to stand by your truth when and where you feel able, for you may be surprised, as I have been, at how many people agree with you.

further reading and resources

The Ancient British Goddess, Kathy Jones, Ariadne, 1991.
British goddesses related to seasonal festivals and landscapes.
This little book is a treasury – lots of pictures and photographs.

The Book of Goddesses and Heroines, Patricia Monaghan,
Llewellyn, 1989.
An invaluable reference book with information on many
goddesses.

The Crone Oracles, Victoria Ransom and Henriette Bernstein,
Weiser, 1994.
The feminine path to wisdom and the ancient tradition of
Eleusis interpreted for today's women and men. This is inspir-
ing, readable and makes sense.

Descent to the Goddess, Sylvia Brinton Perera, Inner City, 1981.
Written by a Jungian, this little book explores the psycho-
logical implications of the myth of Inanna and Ereshkigal.
Interesting.

Eclipse of the Sun, Janet McCrickard, Gothic Image, 1990.
This book describes sun goddesses and moon gods. The author
feels that ancient mythology has been misinterpreted by some

writers and that some goddesses have been repressed. This is
an interesting source book for readers who wish to know more
about sun goddesses.

The Fires of Bride, Ellen Galford, The Womens Press, 1986.
Witty, moving and very significant, this novel tells of the redis-
covery of the goddess on a remote northern island. A good and
memorable read.

Gaia, J.E. Lovelock, Oxford, 1987.
This acclaimed work needs to be read by all those wishing to
understand our planet.

Goddesses for Every Season, Nancy Blair, Element, 1995.
A dear little book, describing a goddess for each week of the
year, with a simple ritual and affirmation, to bring her into your
life.

Grandmother Moon, Zsuzsanna Budapest, Harper (San
Francisco), 1991.
A book of lunar, spells rituals goddesses and emotions. Very
interesting.

Her Blood is Gold, Lara Owen, Aquarian, 1993.
Rediscovering menstruation as creative and magical – the
personal stories of several women are included.

Lady of the Beasts, Buffie Johnson, Inner Traditions
International, 1994.
Revealing and evocative. Recommended.

The Language of the Goddess, Marija Gimbutas, Thames &
Hudson, 1989.
This is a monumental work that has inspired many others.

Large, hardback and illustrated, it details the symbols and history of the Goddess. Recommended.

The Mists of Avalon, Marion Zimmer Bradley, Del Rey, 1982.
A superb and compelling novel about the ancient Goddess worship in Arthurian times.

Mysteries of the Dark Moon, Demetra George, Harper, San Franciso, 1992.
Healing, imaginative and wise, this book explores the rhythms and powers of the menstrual cycle and the dark goddess poetically and mythically, teaching women to reclaim their power.

The Myth of the Goddess, Evolution of an Image, Anne Baring and Jules Cashford, Arkana, 1993.
This is a definitive work, fascinating and far-ranging. Although long it is essential reading.

The Sea Priestess, Dion Fortune, Aquarian, 1989.
One of the foremost occult novels of the century. Other novels by the same author are also worth reading.

The Thirteen Original Clan Mothers, Jamie Sams, HarperCollins, 1994.
Native American feminine wisdom taught gently and inspiringly. A lovely book.

Voices of the Goddess, edited by Caitlin Matthews, Aquarius, 1990.
Moving accounts by priestesses of today.

The Wise Wound, HarperCollins, 1994; *Alchemy for Women*, Rider, 1995; Penelope Shuttle and Peter Redgrove.

Essential reading about the menstrual cycle, its mysteries and meanings.

Witchcraft; The Moon and You for Beginner's; Teresa Moorey, Hodder & Stoughton.
The Wheel of the Year – Myth and Magic Throughout the Seasons, Teresa Moorey and Jane Brideson, Hodder & Stoughton, 1997.
All relevant to current Goddess worship.

The Witches' Goddess, Janet and Stewart Farrar, Phoenix, 1987.
An interesting work on different forms of the Goddess, with rituals to inspire. Alphabetical listing of over 1,000 goddesses. Very useful.

Women in Celtic Myth, Moyra Caldecott, Destiny, 1992.
Old myths brought to life and commented upon. A good read.

Women Who Run With The Wolves, Clarissa Pinkola Estes, Rider, 1993.
By another Jungian author, this is a liberating book, using legends to illustrate the value of the wild side of women and reclaim true feminine power. A galvanising work.

We'moon Diaries
Mother Tongue Inc, PO Box 1395, Estacada, Oregon, USA.
Tel: 503-630-7848.
Each year a diary is compiled from talented contributors, exploring and celebrating Goddess rhythms. This is an invaluable companion through the year.

Useful addresses

N.B. When writing always enclose SAE.

Church of all Worlds
PO Box 408, Woden ACT 2606, Australia. e-mail:
ftswk@cc.newcastle.edu.au

Dark Moon Designs
Selection of cards, lunar calendars and goddess figures – this
book has been illustrated by the same artist.
UK Tel: 01273 623321 for catalogue.

House of the Goddess
33 Oldridge Road, London, SW12 8PN,
UK. Tel: 0208 673 6370.
e-mail i/n hog@goddess.demon.co.uk.
w/w/w. demon.co.uk/goddess.hog (shared with Dragon Environmental Group)

Ganmill Ltd
(Manager Steve Briskham) Personal Hygiene Supplies, Ecofem
Pads, 38 Market Street, Bridgewater, Somerset, TA6 3EP, UK.
Tel: 01278 423037.

Green Egg Magazine
Box 1542, Ukiah, CA 95482, USA.

Moonwit Pads and Liners
Moonwit, R.R. 4 Lang's Road, C-21, Ganges, British Columbia,
Canada VO5 1ED.

New Cycle Products
Menstrual Health Foundation, PO Box 1775, Sebastopol, CA 95473, USA.

The Pagan Federation
BM Box 7097, London, WC1N 3XX, UK. e-mail: Secretary @paganfed.demon.co.uk

Pan-Pacific Pagan Alliance
PO Box 719, Castlemaine 3450, Australia.

Seventh Wave Music
PO Box 1, Totnes, Devon, TQ9 6UQ, UK. Music and poetry expressing our ancient pagan and goddess roots. Some lyrics quoted at chapter headings. Catalogue available.